Margaret Moseley's
A Garden to Remember

Martha Tate

Margaret Moseley's

A Garden to Remember

Martha Tate

BOOKLOGIX®
Alpharetta, GA

Copyright © 2014 by Martha Smith Tate

All rights reserved. No part of this book may be reproduced or transmitted in any form or by any means, electronic or mechanical, including photocopying, recording, or any information storage and retrieval system, without permission in writing from the publisher. For more information, address BookLogix, c/o Permissions Department, 1264 Old Alpharetta Rd., Alpharetta, GA 30005.

10 9 8 7 6 5 4 3 2   0 2 2 0 1 4

Printed in the United States of America

ISBN: 978-1-61005-467-6
Library of Congress Control Number: 2014903512

Designed and illustrated by Mia Broder
www.hedwigd.com

Photography by Martha Tate
www.gardenphotostream.com

Other photographs by Mia Broder, Erica Glasener, and Carolyn Krueger

∞ This paper meets the requirements of ANSI/NISO Z39.48-1992 (Permanence of Paper)

For my dear friend Margaret, whose heart touches everyone she meets and whose soul belongs to every plant she touches.

And in memory of The Hydrangea Lady, Penny McHenry, who graced the gardening world with her kindness.

Table of Contents

Introduction	9
History	15
A Walk Through the Garden	21
Elizabeth Lawrence	41
Collections	47
Viburnums	48
Camellia sasanqua	54
Hydrangeas	62
Camellia japonica	68
Plants Make the Garden	77
Margaret's Plant Combinations	89
Passalong and Heirloom Plants	95
Friends	105
Margaret-isms	117
Hints	127
Finding Health and Happiness in the Garden	133
Index	136

"*I can't believe I planted all that.*"

— *Margaret Moseley, age 97*

For my dear friend Margaret, whose heart touches everyone she meets and whose soul belongs to every plant she touches.

And in memory of The Hydrangea Lady, Penny McHenry, who graced the gardening world with her kindness.

Table of Contents

Introduction	9
History	15
A Walk Through the Garden	21
Elizabeth Lawrence	41
Collections	47
Viburnums	48
Camellia sasanqua	54
Hydrangeas	62
Camellia japonica	68
Plants Make the Garden	77
Margaret's Plant Combinations	89
Passalong and Heirloom Plants	95
Friends	105
Margaret-isms	117
Hints	127
Finding Health and Happiness in the Garden	133
Index	136

"*I can't believe I planted all that.*"

— *Margaret Moseley, age 97*

Introduction

On a spring day in 1994, when I got out of my car at Margaret Moseley's house a few miles east of Atlanta, I knew instantly that I had stumbled upon a magical place. As a garden columnist for the *Atlanta Journal-Constitution* and as co-creator of *A Gardener's Diary,* a series on HGTV (Home & Garden Television), I was always on the lookout for interesting gardens and unconventional characters. That day I found both.

Here, so unexpectedly, was a wondrous garden that contained a stunning array of plants—new introductions that had just hit the market, along with Southern favorites, some of which had long disappeared from retail nurseries.

And, as quickly as I knew this was a very special garden, I could also tell that here was a real character—a seventy-eight-year-old who was full of personality and energy and entertaining stories about how each plant had come to be in her ¾-acre backyard. I was instantly captivated.

By the time I met Margaret, she had been a serious gardener for sixteen years. Although she was obviously a trendsetter, she was unknown to the gardening media. She was reading everything about gardening she could get her hands on and was familiar with my columns in the *Atlanta Journal-Constitution*. She seemed delighted when I asked if I could write about her in the newspaper.

But that first article was a huge disappointment for Margaret, and she let me know it. Oftentimes, my column appeared on the front page of the Home & Garden section, which meant the photographs were in color and prominently displayed. But this time, the piece on Margaret was

1. Margaret's garden in June.
2. Branches of *Viburnum macrocephalum* in its chartreuse stage reach over to a Japanese lantern in one of the "secret gardens." Margaret says this is the only ornament she's ever bought for the garden. The rest were gifts from friends.

practically lost on an inside page, with only two very small black-and-white photographs—one of Margaret's hands around a giant 'Annabelle' hydrangea bloom, the other of a 150-year-old hardy gladiolus. I, too, was crestfallen, as I wanted everyone to recognize that this was a very important garden right here in our own backyard.

It turned out that the placement of the column didn't matter. People caught on, and it wasn't long until Margaret was a celebrity. Garden clubs, plant societies, and Master Gardener groups arrived by the busload for tours.

Other publications caught on, too. Her garden appeared on the cover of *Southern Living* magazine and on their widely distributed book, the *2001 Garden Annual*. Stories about her were published in a *Better Homes and Gardens* special national edition, in *Atlanta Magazine*, and in *Atlanta Homes and Lifestyles*. Two episodes of Home & Garden Television's *A Gardener's Diary*—taped several years apart and at different times of the year—began airing worldwide. Her intriguing garden and her ebullient personality gained her fans from all over the United States and Canada, and from as far away as Japan and Australia.

○···○

Like so many others, I was entranced by Margaret and her magical garden. I devoured her advice, marveled at her plant combinations, studied her unusual collections, and delighted in the funny anecdotes that were in endless supply.

I couldn't stop writing about her because there was a new discovery every week. She truly had a year-round garden, so there was always something to see, even in the dead of winter. One editor finally reprimanded me for mentioning Margaret too much. However, it wasn't long before he was writing big front-

3

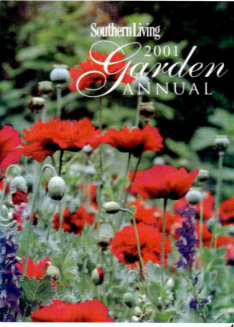
4

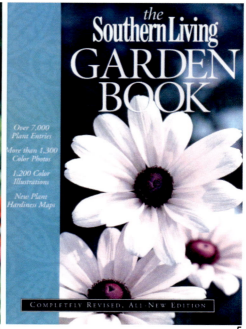
5

HOME & GARDEN

HOME GROWN
MARTHA TATE

Moseley's green magic materializes year-round

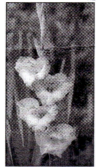

Photos by WILLIAM BERRY / Staff

Hydrangeas (above) and gladioluses (left) brighten Margaret Moseley's garden in June. Each season calls forth something new.

Thirty-three years ago, Margaret Moseley put away the sewing machine she used to make all of her four daughters' clothes, sent her twins off to college and took up gardening on a grand scale.

"I had gardened some," says Moseley, 78, who grew up in Atlanta's East Lake neighborhood, not far from the area of DeKalb County where she lives now. "I would always have some old-fashioned petunias and geraniums. When we moved here in 1965, I started with a 25-foot strip at the side of the house. I'd plant, and then I'd run out of room and clear another little spot, so the garden grew and grew."

Now, three decades later, Moseley's ¾-acre back yard is a draw for plant lovers, who come regularly to see her flower- and shrub-filled borders, some of which measure 100 feet long. Taking inspiration from the writings of Elizabeth Lawrence, Moseley has planted her garden for bloom year-round, incorporating the latest introductions with old garden standbys and heirloom plants like the 135-year-old rose that belonged to her grandmother and an even older hardy gladiolus that was handed down through her husband's family.

"I don't know of much I don't have," Moseley says, "but I'm always thinking about what to plant next, and I never hesitate to move things. I'm lucky, because there used to be a cotton plantation here, so I have good soil to work with."

Much of Moseley's garden grows under a canopy of tall pine trees. Beginning in late fall and through the winter, camellias — one of them more than 20 feet tall — dominate the landscape. In February, there are daffodils, hellebores and daphnes, followed in spring by the blooms of 13 kinds of viburnum. In April, azaleas, lilacs, kerria and broom give way to rhododendrons and iris. In May, peonies, roses, foxgloves and columbine grow in the sunnier beds near the gazebo, while larkspur and poppies are naturalized in a field at the back of the lot.

In June, some 200 kinds of daylilies, alstroemeria, Japanese iris and several spectacular hydrangeas (including an unusual white macrophylla type with a pale blue eye) are followed by lilies, phlox and crocosmia in July. In late summer, there is yet another flush of bloom, with cleomes, boltonia and asters giving way to the fall-blooming plants of September.

Moseley says that part of the joy of her garden is being able to share plants with other gardeners and "never letting anyone go away empty-handed." She also loves entertaining visitors to her garden and cherishes in particular what her minister, the Rev. Walter Jones, said of her work when he came to call last June.

"The garden was in full bloom," Moseley says. "I remember it was about dusk, and he looked out and said, 'Margaret, you have made your own heaven on earth. When you get to the other heaven, the only difference will be you won't have any weeds to pull.'"

COVER STORY
BY DANNY C. FLANDERS / dflanders@ajc.com

3. Margaret's 'Annabelle' hydrangeas on the cover of *Southern Living* magazine, May 2000. The article by Steve Bender was entitled "Flowers Tell the Story."

4. Poppies from Margaret's garden adorned the cover of both the hardback and softbound editions of the *Southern Living 2001 Garden Annual* book.

5. Photographs taken of Margaret and her garden appeared in *The Southern Living Garden Book*, an edition published in 2004.

6. In the summer of 1994, my original column on Margaret was buried within the pages of the Home & Garden section of the *Atlanta Journal-Constitution*. Margaret was disappointed with the placement and the black-and-white photographs, but the story turned out to be far-reaching.

7. This azalea, 'Corsage', a hybrid of the Korean azalea *Rhododendron poukhanense*, is one of the plants I admired on the day I first went to Margaret's garden. The orchid-like flowers are slightly fragrant.

8. A 2002 cover story on viburnums in the *Atlanta Journal-Constitution* featured a full-page photograph of Margaret in her garden. In the background is *Viburnum macrocephalum* coming into bloom.

page feature articles about her and calling her "a garden writer's dream."

○·······························○

Margaret was fifty-two when she started gardening. This fact has served as an inspiration to so many people who had careers and children and no time to spend in a garden. When you would see Margaret out there in her late eighties, adding new plants and expanding beds, you always felt there was hope, that the age you started gardening didn't matter.

For Margaret, who is ninety-seven at the publication of this book, it is never too late to plant or change something in your garden. Just a month ago, she informed me that she was going to dig up a fifteen-foot-tall *Viburnum plicatum* var. *tomentosum* 'Shasta' that I had given her years ago as a tiny stick.

"It's in my front yard, and I want it back here where I can see it," she said. By the time I registered my protest, the plant had already been moved.

○·······························○

So, why have a book entirely devoted to one garden? I say it's for the same reason we featured only one story per episode on *A Gardener's Diary*. Just as a six-or seven-minute walk-through on a television program doesn't give you the whole picture or time to explore the soul of a garden, the same is true here. A few pages on Margaret in a book about several people won't do. There's just too much good material.

However, this is not a conventional garden book. To tell Margaret's story, I have borrowed text from many sources—Margaret's own notes, letters from fans, the stacks of articles that were written about her, testimonials from friends, and from the two episodes of *A Gardener's Diary*.

9. A spread in the May/June 1996 issue of *Atlanta Homes and Lifestyles* magazine showcased Margaret's garden in summer.

10. Garden writers were always looking for stories to run during the winter season. Danny Flanders, garden editor of the *Atlanta Journal-Constitution*, put Margaret and her camellias on the cover of the Home & Garden section in January 2000.

10

Inevitably, Margaret's garden has changed over four decades—big pine trees have fallen, plants have disappeared and been replaced by new varieties, rogue plants have taken over beds. But that special ambience has endured.

In this book, I hope you'll discover the joy Margaret has brought to so many people through her enthusiasm and encouragement, and also the health and happiness Margaret herself has derived from her adventures in creating this beautiful space.

When I took my computer out to show her all the photographs I'd taken of her garden through the years, she stared in amazement: "Oh my," she said. "I can't believe I planted all that."

I couldn't either.

— *Martha Tate*

"When the twins went off to college, I started gardening, and I haven't looked at that sewing machine since."

— *Margaret Moseley*

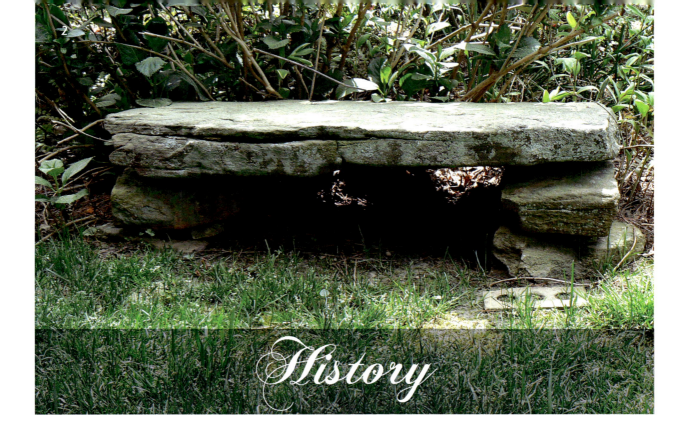

History

Entry from Margaret's Journal:

My love of plants and gardening goes way back. My mother's family was from Veazey, a small community in Greene County, Georgia, about an hour and a half east of Atlanta. Everyone in the country grew flowers. I can remember planting petunias along the long driveway going to my grandmother's house. There were cotton fields on either side. I was given a dipper with a long handle and would draw a bucket of cold water from the well to water the new plants. I'd give each petunia a dipper full of water. I'm sure someone must have come along behind me to make certain the flowers had enough water to survive.

I was born in Greensboro, Georgia, in 1916, but I grew up in DeKalb County, next to Atlanta. From 1933–35, my friend Mildred and I would ride the trolley to Commercial High School on Pryor Street in downtown Atlanta.

During the spring, I would ask Mildred to go over to Hastings with me to look around. Back then, Hastings was a seed store where the farmers bought their seeds and fertilizer. It was not the pretty nursery we know today. It was down on Mitchell Street at that time, and I loved going in there.

1. Margaret inspecting her daylily collection in the late 1960s. The flowers were eventually replaced with a variety of plants.
2. One of the rock benches that came from the foundation of an old house on the property.

Mildred remembers that I once bought a dahlia tuber for five cents and another time a bag of daffodils to take home to my mother. Mildred told me years later that it used to bore her to death to go to Hastings, but she always went with me. Even at the age of eighteen, I had the urge to plant something and watch it grow.

○······················○

I married in 1937, and we moved to East Lake where we raised our four daughters. I liked sitting at the sewing machine, making their clothes, dressing them up for Sunday School, taking them to piano lessons and cheerleading practice. I made every stitch of clothing they wore.

We enjoyed living in East Lake for thirty years, but we wanted more space, so we moved to the country in 1965. We bought one and a half acres that used to be part of a cotton farm.

There was an old house toward the back of the lot where the rose bed is now. It had to be torn down. A friend told us about a man who would take it down for us, and when he came, he had four helpers. We asked them if they could use the best lumber to build us a tool house.

When they cleaned up the trash where the house was, there were two big flat rocks, and I thought about how they could be benches for the yard. The rocks were about four and a half feet long and one and a half feet wide and eight inches deep. I asked the men if they could move them down to where I eventually made my garden.

3. Margaret's graduation picture from Commercial High School in downtown Atlanta, June 3, 1935.
4. Margaret (eight years) and her sister Virginia (six years), circa 1924.
5. L-R Margaret's friend Mildred Cannon, Margaret, Margaret's sister Virginia.

They didn't have the proper equipment, so they rolled them over and over. One of them told me to be sure I knew where I wanted them.

When they got them down, I said, "Joe, I think that one would look better over here." I can't repeat what he said, but we all had a good laugh. I wish those men could see my garden today.

No Garden Yet

This was the country when I first moved here. It was an unpaved road. We would sit out on the porch of the new house and look for cars. Now it is a busy highway with a lot of traffic.

The three-quarters of an acre in back was all blackberries, honeysuckle, and briars. You couldn't even walk back there. It took us a year to clear it.

A Garden from Scratch

After the twins left for college, I was hungry for a hobby. I joined a garden club and took a course in flower arranging. That was for the birds. I tried crocheting, knitting, and needlepoint, but I realized that all I really wanted to do was dig. When I made my decision, I never looked at that sewing machine again.

I was fifty-two years old when I started my garden. I had gardened some in East Lake—old-fashioned petunias, a few geraniums. First, I started with a twenty-five-foot border along the side of the house. Everybody was into daylilies then, and I started a collection.

I had a friend who hybridized daylilies, and she would give me plants. She used to bring her seedlings to see what they'd do the next year. I still have one of her named varieties—'Mary's Gold'.

Every year, the American Hemerocallis Society would choose a new selection for their highest award, the Stout Medal, and I would acquire that flower. I soon had over 300 varieties.

I finally tired of daylilies, because I had too many. I kept my favorites, but gave everything else away.

Then, other friends started sharing different plants. I remember one of the first ones I was given was an old-fashioned hardy begonia (*Begonia grandis*). There were a lot of tall pine trees in back, so I began planting in circles around them. Wherever we would go, I would look for rocks to bring home. If I saw stones on the side of the road, I'd stop and pick them up. Sometimes, it would be freezing cold or raining hard, but I would always gather any rocks I saw. I used them to outline the beds.

Friends continued to share their plants, and when I needed more room, I'd just clean out a spot, add more rocks, and make the beds bigger. That's how I came to have island beds, which just grew and grew. I never had an original plan. The way the garden turned out was just an accident, really.

Spring 1967

The old house is torn down. I have a great tool house, and the trash is cleaned up.

Azaleas are blooming now, so I bought a few to plant around a pine tree. I added a camellia and a rhododendron. There were so many rocks everywhere, I thought I would pick them up and border this bed with them. Of course, I made the bed too small, and I had to pull the rocks out to make more room.

This was the first island bed, and when I filled that up with plants, I started another one.

> **"** I enjoyed my children, and now I enjoy my garden. I don't think anyone can garden and raise four girls. **"**
>
> — Margaret Moseley

6. The tool shed, built with reclaimed lumber when the house was torn down.
7. Margaret used rocks she picked up from the side of the road to outline her beds.
8 Built in the 1960s, Margaret's "house in the country" now stands along a busy road.
9. Hardy begonia (*Begonia grandis*) was one of the first plants given to Margaret by a friend.

" *You should see my garden today. It's the prettiest it's ever been.* "

— *Margaret Moseley*

A Walk Through the Garden

Margaret took us on a tour of her garden, along winding grassy paths that led to one mixed border after another, usually bordered by rocks and each usually set off by a focal point—such as a stone bench that looked very substantial and heavy. There were several plaques, one of which read: "Your feet are killing me," which shows her warm sense of humor and practical side. Also, "My garden is my earthly Paradise."

Seemed it to me.

— A Gwinett County Master Gardener

Margaret basically started with a blank slate—a ¾-acre backyard in the shape of a rectangle. One strip along the north side of the lot is slightly higher than the remainder of the property, which is perfectly flat.

There's no overall view of the entire garden. Any broad vistas are blocked by tall, spreading evergreens in numerous irregular-shaped beds, so you can't always see what is around the next corner. It's like a series of secret gardens.

Garden designer, author, and popular garden blogger Tara Dillard gave a fitting description: "It's old-fashioned garden design nobody does anymore. Her garden is laid out in islands, and her

1. A summer garden scene.
2. Evergreen *Clematis armandii* cascades from the gazebo.

fescue lawn is the Oriental carpet that ties the areas together. Margaret breaks all the rules, but her garden is sublime."

You enter the garden from an area near the door to the sunroom at the back of the house. A double set of pavers separated by dwarf mondo grass passes beneath the branches of a mature ginkgo tree and leads to a water garden straight ahead. Further along is a seating area shaded by a flowering apricot (*Prunus mume*), which has now grown into a tree. A few feet ahead is a Kwanzan cherry tree. From this spot, paths lead to other sections of the garden.

If you turn left, you can make your way up a gentle slope to another level, slightly raised from the main part of the garden. You'll pass 'Annabelle' hydrangeas on one side and boxwoods and a *Camellia sasanqua* on the other. On the raised level, you'll find various shrubs set to bloom throughout the year—rhododendrons, viburnums, *Pieris japonica*, white flowering quince, hydrangeas, purple smoketree, and pearlbush, to name a few.

Back down on the main level and walking under the cherry tree, you'll come to a wide, grassy path that leads past a long, jam-packed flower and shrub border on the left. Although your eye is finally stopped by a line of shrubs (beautybush, kerria, dwarf flowering almond, *Rosa* 'Mutabilis', *Euonymus alatus*, winterhazel, and more viburnums), you can catch a glimpse of the rose garden beyond. In this latter area, you'll see, depending on the season, bearded iris, peonies, a 'Bluebird' althea, sun-loving hydrangeas, and, in fall, bright red pineapple sage.

The wide grass path then takes you by a gazebo draped in evergreen *Clematis armandii*, which is covered in sweet-scented white flowers in March. Next to the wooden structure is the understory

native tree, *Halesia diptera*, with white bells hanging charmingly from the branches in April. Straight ahead, you have a view of the border of the property, which is planted with evergreens—Leyland cypress, camellias, and cherry laurel. A Chinese snowball (*Viburnum macrocephalum*), now a large tree, is a focal point in April with its masses of giant white flowers.

This same path passes between two long, deep beds on either side, all anchored by fifteen- to twenty-foot-tall camellia bushes. Siberian iris, spireas, native azaleas, purple smoketree, baptisias, Florida anise, a pomegranate bush, hardy gladioli, grancy graybeard (*Chionanthus virginicus*), and viburnums—the latter laden with red berries in fall—are just some of the plants you'll see in this area.

If you take a left as you arrive at the end of the border, you'll reach the back of the property where Margaret's fifty-by-sixty-foot poppy patch replaced a vegetable garden. Here, Georgia's state flower, the Cherokee rose (*Rosa laevigata*) forms a huge mound and in spring is covered with single white flowers. In the very back is yet another large *Viburnum macrocephalum*. Forming a flower border in this area is Margaret's collection of David Austin English roses, including 'The Pilgrim', 'Graham Stuart Thomas', and 'Heritage', plus various other roses she's planted.

Doubling back to the main part of the garden, you'll pass more beds of camellias, rhododendrons, and azaleas, all interspersed with seasonal perennials and bulbs and smaller shrubs. A shady glade starts with *Camellia japonica* 'Lady Clare' serving as a backdrop for 'Snowflake' oakleaf hydrangea.

3,4,5. The garden entrance in different seasons: early spring, summer, and winter.

If you glance into a "wild" area along the lot line, you'll see a scramble of plants—daphnes and hellebores, *Scilla hispanica*, Japanese paper plant (*Edgeworthia chrysantha*), Mariana maiden fern, hydrangeas, money plant, with both lavender and white flowers, and Japanese asters.

One path on this side passes next to the tool house. Over the years, Margaret has experimented with various plants here. At one point, the structure was enveloped in evergreen Confederate jasmine. Margaret also planted a bottlebrush buckeye (*Aesculus parviflora*) by the shed, not thinking she would live to see the shrub grow too large for the space. Both plants are gone now, but her original white hydrangea, *H. macrophylla* 'Margaret Moseley' still grows by the door to the shed.

Gardenias are in almost every bed. It's Margaret's rule to have one every twenty-five feet to enjoy the fragrance. Likewise, sweet scented daphnes and fragrant viburnums are planted in many of the island beds. Hidden in these secret passages are stone benches and more hostas and ferns.

If you take the long path outlined with a wide swath of epimediums, you will enter an area where Margaret has part of her hosta collection. Here, among the many beds and paths that lead in all directions, you'll find camellias, sasanquas, rhododendrons, azaleas, hydrangeas, hostas, and ferns.

Margaret does have one vantage point from which she can enjoy a fairly extensive view of part of the garden. Standing inside the glassed-in porch at the back of the house, you can see something going on in every direction. Depending on the season, if

9

you look to the right along the back wall of the house, you can catch a glimpse of three gardenia bushes, two viburnums, and at least three different hydrangeas. Just in front of you, there's a wide swath of yellow creeping Jenny in summer, planted with blue petunias. Huge clumps of hostas, including the giant-leaved 'Sum and Substance', are also in this area.

Further out, at an angle to the right, you'll see the lush green foliage of a 'Butterfly' Japanese maple near the lilac-colored blooms of *Rhododendron* 'Roseum Elegans'. That same view in winter is punctuated by the bright red flowers of *Camellia japonica* 'Governor Mouton'.

Looking straight ahead, a rare *Michelia maudiae*, with creamy magnolia-like flowers in late winter, towers over a bed. Later on in the season, Margaret can watch her bluebird box and monitor all the activity. A rusted iron birdbath in one of the islands has different plantings according to the seasons—*Daphne odora* and the pink *Camellia japonica* 'C. M. Wilson' in winter, blue *Scilla hispanica* in spring, followed by the peach-colored *Iris* 'Beverly Sills' in May. Hydrangeas are visible in all directions. To the left is the entrance, where hellebores, Japanese plum yew, and daphnes grow in the shade of the ginkgo tree.

In fall, the view is of rich green grass and islands filled with colorful *Camellia sasanqua*, and in the distance, the turning leaves of dogwoods. Close to the back window is a stand of white 'Honorine Jobert' Japanese anemones.

6. The wild part of the garden near the southern perimeter of the property.
7. The long border in June.
8. A David Austin English rose in the back border of the garden.

9. Spring bursts forth along a wide path toward the back of the garden. Margaret lined some of her borders with leftover bricks from the construction of her house in the 1960s.

10. One of the rock-lined beds in late winter.
11. As seen from inside the glassed-in porch, dogwoods in the autumn garden.
12. In winter, the blooms of *Camellia japonica* and *Daphne odora* along a winding garden path.
13. Foxgloves (*Digitalis purpurea*) often reseed in the island beds.
14. Clematis are everywhere, climbing in viburnums or on lower-growing shrubs.
15. A lush spring scene as viewed from Margaret's glassed-in sunporch.

Along the driveway on the side of the house, two twenty-foot-tall specimens of *Camellia sasanqua* ('Sparkling Burgundy' and 'Pink Snow') serve as an evergreen screen. In this area in fall, a *Hibiscus mutabilis* (Confederate rose) and Angel's trumpet (*Brugmansia sp.*) add even more color. Outside the kitchen window are a Korean lilac, an Okame cherry tree, and a special sasanqua, 'Martha's Dream'.

Margaret says there's not much going on in the front yard, but she does have the lower-growing *Camellia japonica* 'White By the Gate' and gardenias as foundation plants. Past the columned front porch, one of her favorite trees, *Cornus kousa*, blooms in May. Out in the yard, an *Ilex latifolia* hybrid, 'Emily Brunner', produces loads of bright red berries in winter. Huge specimens of *Hydrangea paniculata* 'Tardiva' create a spectacle in mid-summer.

There are countless other plants all around the garden that ebb and flow with the seasons. In January, you'll find the arrow-shaped, variegated leaves of *Arum italicum* and the pure white blossoms of the Christmas rose (*Helleborus niger*) and Lenten roses (*Helleborus* x *hybridus*) in many of the island beds. The delicate pink blossoms of Margaret's beloved flowering apricot (*Prunus mume*) float above all the blooming camellias.

When spring rolls around again, the viburnums come into bloom, dotting the garden with white and filling it with fragrance. Daffodils and tulips pop up among the blue pansies under the porch window. By May, foxgloves and larkspur appear, followed by hydrangeas, daylilies, garden phlox, and the new fronds of several different kinds of ferns.

And so the seasons continue in this wonderful maze of secret gardens.

16. Margaret loves cats. Here, one of her felines contemplates a swath of *Epimedium* sp. along a hidden path.
17. *Camellia* x 'Taylor's Perfection' frames a grassy path that leads to the back of the garden on the south side.
18. The "iron birdbath" bed, underplanted with *Scilla hispanica* in April.
19. A path leading to secret areas passes beneath the Japanese maple 'Butterfly' on the left.
20. In fall, a leaf-strewn path leads to the long border.

21. Close-up of a bloom on a butterfly bush (*Buddleia davidii*) in summer.
22. In July, the flowers of Abelia chinensis attract a tiger swallowtail butterfly.
23. A hosta in bloom.
24. The pond near the entrance to the garden.

Margaret Moseley's Garden Overview

A Guide to Margaret Moseley's Garden

   Hydrangea

Fern   Viburnum

Hosta Camellia

Iris   Gardenia

Perennials Azalea

Annuals   Rhododendron

Shrubs   Daphne

 Grass Path
 Upper Level
Beds
Long Border
Wild Garden

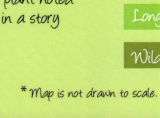
A plant noted in a story

* Map is not drawn to scale.

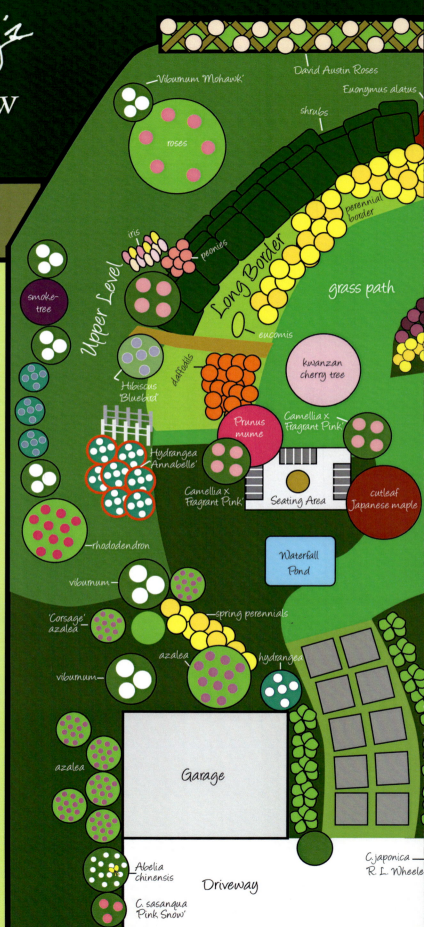

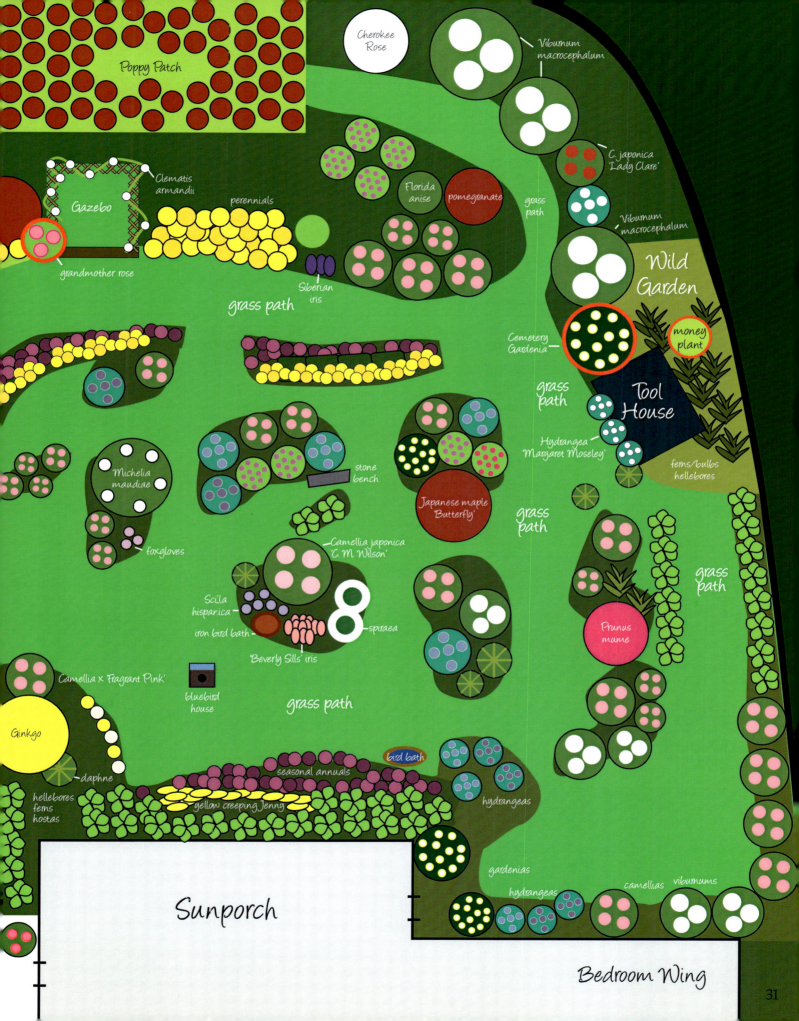

25. Seen here in April, the wide path at the back of the garden is flanked by flower and shrub borders on either side.
26. In May, *Baptisia alba* blooms in a perennial and shrub border near the back of the garden.
27. The pink form of dwarf flowering almond (*Prunus glandulosa*) grows in the shrub border next to the rose garden. The light yellow flowers in back hang from the branches of a corylopsis, or winterhazel.
28. The long border in late winter. A bell jar given to Margaret by noted gardener Susanne Hudson of Douglasville, Georgia, covers a tender plant.

29. Hidden along a path near the back of the garden is *Hydrangea quercifolia* 'Snowflake', backed by the foliage of *Camellia japonica* 'Lady Clare'.
30. *Itea virginica* 'Henry's Garnet' produces white panicles in late April. In fall, the leaves of this native plant turn scarlet and crimson.
31. *Rhododendron* 'Anna Rose Whitney' anchors one end of the upper level garden.
32. In the front yard, a hybrid of *Ilex latifolia* ('Emily Brunner') provides loads of red berries in winter.

33. A June grouping, as seen from the sunporch, includes views of some of the many hydrangeas planted around the garden.

34. The native silverbell (*Halesia diptera*) is one of Margaret's favorite understory trees.

35. The view from Margaret's sunporch in winter reveals the structural elements of the garden—beautiful bark, evergreen foliage, bird baths, and a lush green lawn.
36. Bearded iris bloom next to the rose garden.
37. A lacecap hydrangea grows at the corner of one of the pillars of the carport.
38. A shaggy poppy in the large patch at the very back of the lot.

39. Margaret has planted fragrant daphnes in several beds around the garden. The plants bloom in February.
40. Hellebores are planted all throughout the garden. The blooms start as early as January and hold on until early May.
41. In the upper level of the garden, Margaret planted a purple smoketree (*Cotinus coggygria* 'Royal Purple') to contrast with a lime-colored spirea.
42. In this late November scene, the evergreen Japanese plum yew forms a low border. Beyond, you can make out the red flowers of *Camellia sasanqua* 'Yuletide'.

43. The delicate flowers of a lacecap hydrangea float above muted green foliage in the June garden. To the right is one of Margaret's many gardenias.

> *My greatest influence was Elizabeth Lawrence. How I adore her books. She was a down-to-earth gardener and writer. I could read her all day.*

— *Margaret Moseley*

Elizabeth Lawrence

HOW MARGARET BECAME THE VERY PERSON SHE SO ADMIRED

Margaret's greatest inspiration was the garden writer Elizabeth Lawrence. Margaret loved the way the renowned author of books and newspaper columns wrote about how plants performed in her North Carolina garden and about the people who had shared knowledge and plants with her.

Margaret first discovered a copy of Elizabeth Lawrence's *A Southern Garden: A Handbook for the Middle South* (The University of North Carolina Press) at a used bookstore on St. Simons Island, Georgia. The book captivated Margaret, and she kept the copy on her nightstand, reading it over and over and making copious notes in the margins.

"How I adore that book," she said on an episode of *A Gardener's Diary* on Home & Garden Television. "Elizabeth Lawrence is a down-to-earth gardener and writer. She tells me about her friends, where she gets her plants, and how they do in her garden. I could read her for hours on end."

Elizabeth Lawrence was a garden writer from North Carolina, and her books, written in the mid-twentieth century (*A Southern Garden* was first published in 1942), gained popularity in the 1980s. She wrote some 700 columns about gardening for *The Charlotte Observer*. Margaret went on to collect all of Elizabeth Lawrence's books and loved reading passages to friends and quoting the noted writer.

1. From *A Southern Garden* by Elizabeth Lawrence. Copyright © 1942 by the University of North Carolina Press, renewed 1970 by Elizabeth Lawrence. New preface © 1984 by the University of North Carolina Press. Used by permission of the publisher. http://www.uncpress.unc.edu/.
2. A rustic birdhouse set against *Camellia japonica* 'Governor Mouton'. During the summer, the same birdhouse presides over *Hydrangea* x 'Prezicsa'.

Taking inspiration from *A Southern Garden*, Margaret planted her own garden for bloom year round. She incorporated the latest introductions with old garden standbys and heirloom plants like the 135-year-old rose that belonged to her grandmother and an even older hardy gladiolus that has been handed down through another branch of her family.

Margaret also swapped plants and was responsible for introducing many varieties to the Atlanta area. It was through Margaret that many local gardeners came to know the white Japanese aster, *Kalimeris pinnatifida* 'Hortensis', which Elizabeth Lawrence had saved from obscurity. Countless other flowers bloom in area gardens because Margaret made it known they were worth growing.

In 1994, I wrote a feature article for *Atlanta Homes and Lifestyles* magazine. After reading my notes from interviews and visits with Margaret, I wrote:

"Perhaps the real charm of Margaret's garden stems from her unabashed enjoyment of her creation. Friends often receive calls, even in the dead of winter, saying, 'You ought to see my garden today. It's the prettiest it's ever been.' On summer afternoons, when it is too hot to work, Margaret strolls around her backyard, sipping her famous almond iced tea and, maybe without realizing it, living out a passage from her well-worn copy of Elizabeth Lawrence's *A Southern Garden*:

"'I think of a garden not as a manifestation of spring (like an Easter hat) nor as beds of flowers to be cut and brought into the house, but as a place to be in and enjoy every month of the year.'"

Ironically, Margaret ended up doing exactly what her mentor had done. She told stories about where her plants had come from (she remembered every single person who'd ever brought her a cutting or a division) and told how the plants did in her garden. She corresponded with gardeners who bought her seeds through the *Farmers and Consumers Market Bulletin* and made innumerable friends with people who had seen her on television or read about her in the newspaper.

For many of us, Margaret became our own Elizabeth Lawrence, instilling in us a love for gardening, sharing her plants and advice, and, most of all, showing us that one person could create a place of great happiness and beauty and enjoy every minute of it.

3. The frothy white flowers of *Kalimeris pinnatifida* 'Hortensis', the Elizabeth Lawrence aster, grow in several places in Margaret's garden. Seen here paired with *Hydrangea arborescens* 'Annabelle'.

The Purloined Book

Margaret Moseley was always so generous with her flowers and willing to share what she had. One February in the mid-1990s, she dug up a clump of gorgeous, pure white Lenten roses (*Helleborus* x *hybridus*; formerly *H. orientalis*) so I could use them in a display at the Southeastern Flower Show. She also lent me her antique teapot, which she used for brewing her almond tea, some silver spoons, and her treasured copy of *A Southern Garden* by Elizabeth Lawrence. Margaret had years' worth of notes she'd made in the margins of her cherished book. The copy was worn, but it contained Margaret's observations on her own garden. She had underlined passages she liked and circled plants she wanted to try. It was one of her greatest treasures.

I had placed the book, along with her grandmother's teapot and the spoons, on an antique iron table in the display garden we created for *A Gardener's Diary*, representing four gardens we had featured on Home & Garden Television. In Margaret's section were camellias, rocks she'd picked up from the roadside to create her raised beds, daphnes, the pure white hellebores, and fragrant viburnums. A sign explained the garden and told of Margaret's admiration for Elizabeth Lawrence's writings. The book was opened to the section, "Spring Comes in February."

One morning when I reported for duty at the display, I looked over and saw that Margaret's book was gone. The teapot and the spoons were there, but no book. We looked for it everywhere and couldn't imagine how it could have disappeared. I kept thinking someone had borrowed it to read and would bring it back.

But after a day of asking everyone nearby, hope began to fade.

By the end of the show, the book had still not turned up. I had to face the fact that Margaret's most cherished possession had been stolen.

What puzzles me is this was not a pretty coffee table book. It was a small, tattered paperback with markings all over the inside. A person would have had to climb into the display in order to take it. Only someone who appreciated Elizabeth Lawrence's writings or who knew about Margaret Moseley's garden would have wanted such a marked-up copy. But then, such a person surely would not steal anything, much less something of obvious personal and sentimental value.

I felt so bad. I, too, had this edition and had written and underlined all through it. I could easily have used my own book, but who would have thought? I gave my copy to Margaret, and as the word got out, she received many other copies from friends.

Margaret brushed off the incident, saying it didn't matter a bit, and insisted that I bring the clump of hellebores home and plant them in my garden.

Every winter when those flowers come into bloom (I have other white Lenten roses, but they have freckles, not pure white like Margaret's), I cringe to think about what happened. It was so generous of Margaret to dig those flowers from her garden to use in the display and then insist I take them home with me. I just wish I could have taken better care of her book.

— *Martha Tate*

4. Pure white Lenten roses (*Helleborus* x *hybridus*) still grow in Margaret's garden. Flowers grown from seed will not all be the same, but the original plant will not change.

5. "This blue pitcher belonged to my grandmother. I remember she would keep it by her side at the dinner table," recalls Margaret.

Recipe for Almond Tea:

Margaret loved serving her special iced tea to visitors to the garden. After the tea was featured on HGTV's *A Gardener's Diary*, Margaret received requests for the recipe from all over the world.

7 cups water

1 cup sugar

2/3 cup fresh lemon juice
(approximately 5 lemons)

2 teaspoons almond flavoring

1 teaspoon vanilla flavoring

2 large family-sized tea bags

Boil water, dissolve sugar. Add tea bags.
Add lemon juice and flavorings.
Chill and pour over ice.

" *I'd get so excited about a plant, I'd just have to have it. Then I'd have to go to bed to think about where to plant it.* "

— *Margaret Moseley*

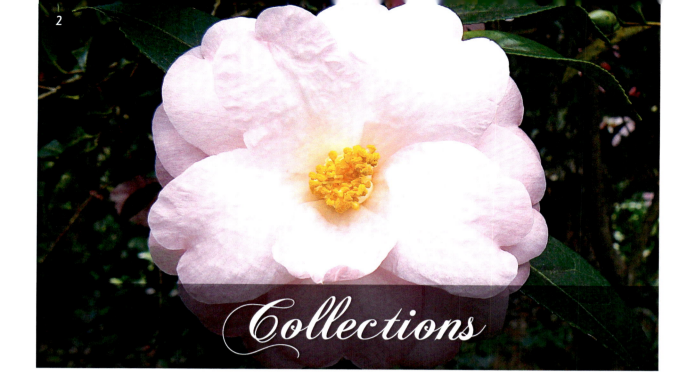

Collections

HOW SHE STARTED A GARDEN FROM SCRATCH

One way Margaret built her garden was by collections. She would fall in love with a genus of plants, and, after she was hooked, she'd launch a search for varieties she didn't have.

"It's the best way to start a garden," she says. "It's like a treasure hunt. And, if you collect both deciduous and evergreen shrubs, then you'll have a good mix and can work from there."

Margaret, a self-taught gardener, had an innate ability to picture how a plant would appear and how it should be used to its best advantage. She realized early on that deciduous shrubs (those that lose their leaves in winter) should be backed by evergreens so the garden would have structure in winter. This meant that the four collections which form the backbone of her garden—viburnums, *Camellia sasanqua*, *Camellia japonica*, and hydrangeas—all complement one another.

For a beginner with a blank palette, using collections to organize and build a garden can be invaluable, she says. Plus, you have the thrill of the chase in acquiring different cultivars. It certainly worked for Margaret.

1. One of Margaret's favorite camellias, 'C. M. Wilson', forms the backdrop for her cherished iron birdbath, a gift from her friend Phyllis McGuinn. As for the camellia, Margaret says: "I don't know of anything any prettier."
2. *Camellia japonica* 'Berenice Boddy'.

Viburnums

March 18, 1998

Dear Martha,

The years fly by. Doesn't seem like any time since my garden was like a perfume factory—my beloved viburnums—how I love them. We can't have too many.

Love,

Margaret

1. *Viburnum macrocephalum* (Chinese snowball).
2. *Viburnum dilatatum* 'Erie' (linden viburnum) with fall fruit.
3. *Viburnum dilatatum* 'Erie' in flower.

Entry from Margaret's Journal:

March 15, 2003

My four favorite viburnums are in full bloom, and the fragrance is over the entire garden. It all started in St. Simons Island on the coast of South Georgia.

I would go there three or four times a year after the children had gone off to college. I loved staying at the King and Prince Hotel so much. In January of 1968, I went over to the village to the used bookstore where I spent a lot of time, and I met an avid gardener from Atlanta. She and her husband had just finished their new home on St. Simons.

She told me she would invite me to see her garden in Atlanta when they got home. She called me in March, and I went over, and as I walked in her house, I caught the most wonderful fragrance. I asked her what it was, and she told me to come to the garden and she would show me. There was the prettiest shrub in bloom with a fragrance I couldn't believe. It was *Viburnum carlesii*, the Korean spice viburnum.

About two weeks later, I received a package from Wayside Gardens. In it was a *Viburnum carlesii*. I called Elizabeth and thanked her for it, and she told me not to plant it until she came out the next day.

I had just started my garden, so she chose the north side of the house near the back door so we could enjoy the fragrance. It is in full bloom today and is as beautiful as she was. Two years later, she and her husband were down at their new home in St. Simons, and she had a heart attack and died at fifty-nine years old. She is buried at Christ Church cemetery on the island she loved.

Elizabeth introduced me to viburnums, and through the years, I have collected seventeen different ones. I especially love the fragrant ones like 'Mohawk', juddii, and carlcephalum. They are all so beautiful.

4. Trying to get Margaret to name a favorite fragrant viburnum is like asking her to pick a favorite child. When pressed, she says *V. carlesii*, the Korean spice viburnum, may have the most delicious scent of all plants in this group. She believes that viburnums are overlooked by Southern gardeners. "I just don't know why more people don't plant them."

5. *Viburnum* × *carlcephalum* is the last of Margaret's fragrant snowballs to come into bloom. Thick pink buds open into semi-globes of fragrant flowers. Margaret often grows clematis on this shrub, due to its open habit. The flowers of *V.* × *carlcephalum* are larger than most of the other fragrant forms.

6. *Viburnum* × *burkwoodii* 'Mohawk'. A fragrant viburnum with a strong, spicy perfume. In autumn, its foliage turns a brilliant orange-red. In 1993, 'Mohawk' won the Pennsylvania Horticultural Society's Gold Medal Plant Award.

7. Margaret, holding a branch of *Viburnum plicatum forma* 'Popcorn', with Michael A. Dirr. Dr. Dirr discovered this heat and drought tolerant and very floriferous shrub on a trip to England in 1999. When he invited Margaret to see his trial gardens near Athens, Georgia, she was thrilled. In Margaret's copy of his book, *Viburnums: Flowering Shrubs for Every Season* (Timber Press), he wrote:

"Dear Margaret,
    Gardeners never grow old...the future is always more exciting than the past. Pleased to know that there are two viburnum lovers in this world.

                      My best,
                      Michael A. Dirr
                      4-22-08, Athens, Georgia"

8. *Viburnum utile* 'Eskimo': This compact snowball viburnum was introduced by the National Arboretum in Washington, DC, in 1981. Because it blooms later than the giant snowball *Viburnum macrocephalum*, the shrub can withstand colder temperatures that occur in states like Kentucky. Growing to about five feet high and as wide, this viburnum is ideal for smaller gardens. A cross between *Viburnum utile* and *V.* × *carlcephalum* 'Cayuga', 'Eskimo' is very showy in spring. Margaret placed 'Eskimo' against the beautiful dark evergreen foliage of *Camellia japonica* 'Lady Clare'.

9. *Viburnum plicatum* var. *tomentosum* 'Shasta' (doublefile viburnum). The lacy blooms are pure white; a good shrub to extend the dogwood season.

10. *Viburnum macrocephalum* (Chinese snowball). Margaret's original shrub has now been limbed up into a tall flowering tree. This is the largest and showiest of all the snowball viburnums, with giant sterile flowers that sometimes measure eight inches across. Some years, the shrub blooms again in September and October. Margaret has three others of this species planted at the back of the garden. "It's very easy to grow, and everybody ought to have one," says Margaret.

11. Fall fruit of the tea viburnum (*Viburnum setigerum*).

12. *Viburnum macrocephalum* in its apple green stage: As the flowers form in early spring, small domes are vivid green. As the season progresses, the domes become round balls and go through a mint green stage before turning pure white. The shrub is often mistaken for an early blooming hydrangea.

13. Margaret bought what was supposed to be *Viburnum plicatum* 'Kern's Pink' when my article about the plant came out in the *Atlanta Journal-Constitution*. The flowers never turned pink, however, and were instead a sickly gray-brown. For years, Margaret threatened to cut the shrub down (she did get her money back from the nursery). Finally, the flowers bloomed pure white, and the shrub was spared.

Camellia sasanqua

(The following was written from notes I took for my column in the Atlanta Journal-Constitution. — Martha Tate*)*

A call came one Friday in October: "You've got to see these sasanquas." When I drove up to Margaret's house and walked into the backyard, it was startling. So much color at a time when other gardens were looking tired. Flowers, mostly in pastel hues, smothered numerous dark green shrubs, many of them fifteen feet tall.

While *Camellia japonica* is the star of Margaret's winter garden, it is her collection of the species *Camellia sasanqua* that makes her fall garden look so colorful and vibrant. During the months of October and November, the sasanquas are at their peak. While you see the leaves of hostas beginning to turn golden and the stands of Japanese Solomon's seal taking on a lemony translucence, Margaret has planted so many varieties of *Camellia sasanqua* throughout the garden that the whites and pastels give you a feeling of the freshness of spring.

For decades, *Camellia sasanqua*, once a Southern favorite, had fallen out of favor. But not in Margaret's garden. While enthusiasts of *Camellia japonica* have often viewed sasanquas as valuable only as understock for grafting the larger flowering *Camellia japonica*, Margaret recognized that sasanquas were beautiful in their own right. Including these evergreen shrubs has helped in her quest to create a year-round garden.

Her collection includes cultivars like 'Cleopatra', 'Cotton Candy', 'Jean May', 'Mine-No-Yuki' (also known as 'Snow' and 'White Doves'), 'Pink Snow', 'Setsugekka', 'Sparkling Burgundy', 'Pink Icicle' (actually a hybrid, but in bloom in fall), and 'Leslie Ann'.

The 'Pink Snow' planted along the driveway looks like a fountain of pink, with branches laden with flowers cascading down from a twenty-foot-tall shrub. Next to it, 'Sparkling Burgundy', a later bloomer, displays thousands of buds on an enormous plant. These sasanquas also serve to screen Margaret's driveway from the neighbor's yard.

Some of the early species begin blooming in September, but most of the shrubs are at their peak during October and November, even lasting into December. The colors range from

the purest white (*C. sasanqua* 'Martha's Dream') to clear pink ('Jean May') to mauve ('Sparkling Burgundy') to bright red ('Yuletide'). Many of the sasanquas are newer introductions and have larger blooms or picotee edging ('Leslie Ann'—white with a pink outline).

The shrubs, which have smaller leaves than those of *Camellia japonica*, not only flower profusely, but they provide dark green backgrounds

1. 'Cotton Candy' is one of the stars of Margaret's fall garden. "It is always loaded with flowers," says Margaret. "It's beautiful every year and blooms over a long period of time."
2. *Camellia* x 'Pink Icicle' is not a sasanqua, but it blooms in late fall. It is hardier than most sasanquas, to Zone 6B.
3, 4. *Camellia sasanqua* 'Yuletide' is probably the brightest colored of all the species. Very showy in the garden.

5. *Camellia sasanqua* 'Setsugekka' is also known as 'Fluted White'.
6. 'Pink Snow' cascades like a fountain along the driveway.
7. In a fall scene, *Camellia sasanqua* 'Mine-No-Yuki' (also called 'White Doves') combines beautifully with the dark green boxwood and the faded flowers and foliage of hydrangeas.
8. *Camellia sasanqua* 'Leslie Ann'.

for deciduous shrubs that flower in spring. Some sasanquas like 'Yuletide' have a dense, compact habit. Others are looser and can appear to cascade and form pink or white fountains. The open forms are particularly useful for espaliers.

Margaret says sasanquas are not good candidates for foundation plantings and recommends planting them where they will not have to be pruned.

"I knew better, but I planted 'Martha's Dream' next to the house. We had to cut half of it down one year. I was just sick. But I should never have planted it here where it didn't have enough room. It turned out that cutting it back didn't hurt the plant, though."

9. *Camellia sasanqua* 'Martha's Dream' is one of Margaret's favorites, but she says the plant is now difficult to find in the nursery trade.

10. This beautiful hybrid camellia, C. x 'Showa-No-Sakae', blooms in fall along with the sasanquas. It was named in honor of Emperor Hirohito of Japan (1901–1989) and means Glory of the Showa, Showa indicating the Era of Enlightened Peace, beginning with the ascent of the emperor in 1926. This latter is ironic given the ensuing events of World War II. The plant is actually a very old Chinese-Japanese hybrid, which was brought to Europe by Dutch traders in the mid-nineteenth century. It was officially named in Japan in 1928. Some of the flowers on Margaret's shrub are semi-double with bright yellow stamens. Others are very double, much like peonies.

11. 'Cotton Candy' is a popular sasanqua and widely available.

12. Sasanquas and camellias dot the landscape in a view from the upper garden.

Hydrangeas

Long before she met Penny McHenry, founder of the American Hydrangea Society, Margaret, who was a charter member of the society, had collected hydrangeas. Most of Margaret's early specimens, which are planted throughout the garden, were given to her by friends. As a result, the exact cultivar names are uncertain.

Margaret collected many types of hydrangeas—both mophead and lacecap forms of *Hydrangea macrophylla* (sometimes called French hydrangeas or bigleaf hydrangea), *Hydrangea serrata* (notably 'Bluebird' and 'Preziosa'), *Hydrangea arborescens* 'Annabelle' (Margaret's have notoriously large blooms), oakleaf hydrangeas (*H. quercifolia*), the sun-loving *Hydrangea paniculata*, and climbing hydrangeas (*Schizophragma hydrangeoides* 'Moonlight' and the native *Decumaria barbara*).

For years, Margaret's garden was on the American Hydrangea Society's annual tour in June. She and Penny McHenry (whose 'Penny Mac' is in gardens all over the country, along with the compact form, 'Mini Penny', selected by Michael A. Dirr) were always joking with each other about their popularity. The two "grandes dames" of Atlanta gardening would often appear together at nurseries or at lectures to promote hydrangeas.

"I already had hydrangeas when I heard about Penny McHenry," explains Margaret. "I went to see her, and we became the closest of friends."

It was Margaret who first influenced Penny to add other shrubs like camellias and daphnes to carry Penny's garden through the winter, and ferns and hostas to complement the enormous hydrangea collection in summer.

"I wish I'd met her thirty years ago," Penny said when Margaret, now ninety-seven, was eighty years old.
"She had such vision. She knew to plant all of these things that I'm just now figuring out to put in my garden."

1. Margaret is known for the size of the blooms on her *Hydrangea arborescens* 'Annabelle'. In late February, she cuts the plants back to about eighteen inches to encourage large, soccer-ball-sized blooms. She prunes the *Hydrangea paniculata* bushes at the same time. Both species bloom on new wood.

2. *Hydrangea macrophylla* 'Twist-n-Shout' is a cross between the mophead 'Penny Mac' and the lacecap 'Lady in Red'. Margaret's shrub was a gift from Michael A. Dirr, who introduced the cultivar. Although most of the blooms are now blue on Margaret's plant, during the first two years, she had flowers ranging from mauve to bright pink to lavender.

Margaret's account of the story of the mysterious "white hydrangea."

"When we were living over at East Lake, I was at Green Brothers Nursery, which no longer exists, and saw this small white hydrangea in bloom. The tag said only 'White Hydrangea.'

"At the time, we didn't have white hydrangeas around here. I paid $2 for the plant.

"When we moved to our new house in 1965, I dug the plant up and brought it with me. I planted it over by the tool house. From that one plant, I don't know how many I've given away. It's a good one because it blooms whether you trim it or not."

The true identity of Margaret's white hydrangea remains a mystery. It's definitely some form of *Hydrangea macrophylla*, but it is not 'Sister Theresa', nor is it 'Mme. Émile Moulière'. It blooms early and prolifically with small-to-medium-sized, pure white flowers that develop a light blue eye in the center of each floret.

Elizabeth Dean and Gene Griffith at Hydrangea.com and the owners of Wilkerson Mill Gardens, a specialty nursery near Palmetto, Georgia, are propagating the plant to introduce to the trade. The shrub will be known as *Hydrangea macrophylla* 'Margaret Moseley'.

In the words of Tara Dillard, garden blogger, designer, and author of garden books: "If something blooms every year in your garden for nearly fifty years, you know you've got a good plant."

3. The white *Hydrangea macrophylla* 'Margaret Moseley' develops a blue "eye" in the center of each floret as the blooms mature.
4. Margaret planted sun-loving forms of *Hydrangea paniculata*, which bloom in July and August. In the foreground is 'Tardiva'. Seen in the distance is 'Grandiflora'.
5. Many of Margaret's hydrangeas were gifts from friends, and the names of the selections remain unknown. In turn, Margaret has layered (propagated by laying down a branch and securing it to the ground) many of her hydrangeas to give to friends.
6. Climbing hydrangea *Schizophragma hydrangeoides* 'Moonlight' billows from the remains of a pine tree.

7. *Hydrangea serrata* 'Fuji Waterfall' is an unusual lacecap form with sterile flowers that are double.
8. One of Margaret's mophead hydrangeas is shown here with the fruits of *Prunus mume* (flowering apricot), a favorite small tree that flowers in January.
9. The flowers of May-blooming *Hydrangea quercifolia* (oakleaf hydrangea) turn from white to mottled pink and green as the season progresses.

Camellia japonica

Entry from Margaret's Journal:

Christmas Eve 2002

The children came yesterday because I wanted them to see the three Christmas trees in the garden. The red one is *Camellia japonica* 'Professor Charles S. Sargent', about eighteen feet tall, and when the sun is shining on it, it is so beautiful. I should have added a big red bow. Next year I will. At the base of this camellia is a bed of holly fern, which is evergreen.

The white one is my favorite, 'White Empress', and across the path from this one is 'Lady Clare', just loaded with blooms. 'Lady Clare' does not grow in the shape of a Christmas tree, but it's a beautiful big shrub with rose pink flowers.

The other one is *Camellia japonica* 'Debutante', a light pink one that must have 500 blooms.

Across the path is 'Daikagura', which has been blooming since October. I have the solid rose-colored form and the one splotched with white. This is the only japonica that I know of that blooms in the fall and blooms through February. The ground cover under this one is *Arum italicum* that is about a foot high now. This is a beautiful winter plant for the shade garden. It dies down in the hot weather, and then *Hosta* 'Blue Angel' and maidenhair ferns take over.

All of these camellias are early- to mid-season bloomers. I don't remember but one year that I didn't have a 'White Empress' in the house for Christmas.

The bed in the center of the garden that gets more sun than the others is pretty now with my favorite 'Azure Blue' pansies. I'm so lucky to have them. My minister's wife, Jeane Jones, knew that I had not had them for two years. She called me in October from Montreat, North Carolina, and asked me if I had found them this year, and I told her no, I had not. She said they were coming home tomorrow, and she was bringing me some. What a friend, and when she got here the next day, and I saw those pansies already blooming, I was so excited. I got them in the ground the next morning, and what fun I had. I wish Jeane could see them today. She will be here later, and they will be even prettier.

Across the path, I planted my new deep pink sasanqua—'Kanjiro'—so pretty with the pansies. The garden is lovely today with the green winding paths, but after tomorrow, it may not be, as cold weather is coming.

1. *Written from an interview by Martha Tate one February:*

A couple of weeks ago, Margaret asked me to come and look at one of her most prized plants, the very unusual hybrid, *Camellia* x 'Fragrant Pink'. Standing in Margaret's newly decorated garden room (a converted carport with windows that look out onto her backyard), I couldn't believe what I saw.

Looking past the bluebird box and out into the garden, it looked like the month of May had already arrived. There were several specimens of the familiar *Camellia japonica* contributing to the scene (among others, two giant, rounded bushes of the red 'Governor Mouton' and the exquisite clear pink of 'Taylor's Perfection'). There were also several fragrant daphnes smothered with flowers and a fabulous *Pieris japonica* dripping with snow-white racemes.

But what gave Margaret's garden the appearance of May was 'Fragrant Pink', a type of camellia that is a cross between *Camellia lutchuensis* and *Camellia rusticana*. Several bushes of varying heights were loaded with double rose-like blossoms growing along the entire length of the branches.

"Everybody who comes here wants this shrub," Margaret said. "From a distance, it looks like a rose bush in full bloom. I like everything about it. Even after the flowers are gone, the new foliage is a gorgeous bronzy-red. It just adds so much to the garden year-round."

Introduced in 1975 by W. L. Ackerman from Glenn Dale, Maryland, 'Fragrant Pink' has medium pink, peony-form flowers, which, although almost miniature, are clustered in great profusion all along the branches of the plant. The habit of the shrub is rather open. Some branches appear to weep, revealing the habit of the *C. lutchuensis* parent. The same parent also lends a subtle rose fragrance to the flowers of the hybrid. The evergreen leaves are dark glossy green.

2. Margaret grows both 'Daikagura' and the solid 'Daikagura Pink' form. Both begin blooming in fall, ahead of the other japonicas.

3. *Camellia japonica* 'White Empress' first bloomed in the US in 1939 and was introduced commercially in 1943. The vigorous plant eventually grows into a dense, evergreen cone. The large buds open into pure white, semi-double flowers with yellow stamens. The large, tapered leaves are glossy and evergreen.

4. 'White By the Gate' is in front of Margaret's house. It originated in Louisiana. The formal double blooms are the purest white. This shrub doesn't grow as tall as other camellias, but Margaret does keep hers trimmed back. She normally advises not to plant camellias as foundation plants against the house. She made an exception for 'White By the Gate'. The camellias in her backyard are like big trees, although she lets the foliage come all the way to the ground.

5. *Camellia japonica* 'Magnoliaeflora' is also known as 'Hagoromo', 'Rose of Dawn', and 'Cho-No-Hagasan'. 'Magnoliaeflora' came from Japan via Italy in 1886 and is an old-fashioned, popular variety. With all the thousands of camellias introduced since, it remains one of the most beautiful and desirable camellias for the southeastern United States.

Entry from Margaret's Journal:

January 2003

This has been the coldest January I have ever seen—below freezing every night. The blooms on all the camellias have been killed, but there are still a lot of buds that will bloom later.

My favorite day trip that I look forward to is going to the American Camellia Society Headquarters at Massee Lane near Fort Valley, Georgia. In the mid-nineties, my friends—Sandra Jonas, Penny McHenry, and Tara Dillard—and I went down. As we drove in the driveway, there was the prettiest shrub in full bloom that I have ever seen. It looked more like a shrub rose bush than a camellia. I stopped the car, and Tara went over to see if it had a tag. It was 'Fragrant Pink'.

At that time, they didn't sell plants at the display gardens. The next day, I called every nursery in Atlanta, and I finally found it at Walker Nursery Farms in Jonesboro.

I love the plant. It blooms from January to April, and now even in the cold weather, mine are blooming. I have five in my garden because they add so much color during the winter.

Entry from Margaret's Journal (Undated):

I think I like the late blooming camellias better than the early varieties. 'Miss Bessie Beville', 'C. M. Wilson', and 'Taylor's Perfection' are in full bloom now. I was down at American Camellia Headquarters with some friends in January about five years ago and saw 'C. M. Wilson'. At that time, they were selling plants at the garden, and I brought one home. I think this is the prettiest *Camellia japonica* I have ever seen.

The *Prunus mume* is in full bloom, and, and oh, the 'Fragrant Pink' looks like a fountain, and 'Lady Clare' is loaded with flowers. I wish everybody could see 'White By the Gate'. I've just picked all the blooms so they won't freeze.

6. 'Lady Clare' is an antique camellia brought to England from Japan in 1887. It has rose-colored flowers with prominent yellow stamens. The leaves are large and dark and exceedingly beautiful, making this a plant that looks good in mid-summer. Its other name is 'Empress'. Margaret has the white form and has issued the following advice for years: "If you see 'White Empress', buy it. You may never see it for sale again. It's hard to find."

7. 'Taylor's Perfection' is a japonica hybrid from New Zealand. One can understand why it has "perfection" in its name. The color is clear pink. The flowers are truly dazzling when they open up and are so finely formed that they appear almost artificial.

8. *Camellia japonica* 'Governor Mouton' is hard to find these days, but it has grown in Margaret's garden for forty years.

9. *Camellia* x 'Tiny Princess' is a japonica hybrid introduced in 1961. The flowers are miniature with a semi-double form.

10. Margaret found *Camellia japonica* 'James Hyde Porter' at her local branch of Pike Family Nurseries, which was on her circuit of garden centers she visited regularly.

" *The only way you can get to know plants is to handle them yourself.* "

— *Margaret Moseley*

Plants Make the Garden

Although she never had a master plan, plants—not hardscapes nor garden ornaments—have been responsible for the year-round beauty of Margaret's garden. Her plant material is vast and varied and includes both old and new cultivars of perennials, shrubs, vines, bulbs, and small trees.

Margaret is a self-taught gardener. She read books and magazines and studied catalogs, looking for plants that interested her. She visited nurseries when things were in bloom, so she could judge for herself whether something would work in the garden. She got to know employees at the nurseries, so she could find out if anything interesting had come in.

Tara Dillard, an author of books on garden design and a popular blogger who claims Margaret as her mentor, explains how she came under Margaret's spell:

"Did I tell you how I met Margaret? Every Friday, she came into Hall's Garden Center, where I worked. I loved talking with her. Kelvin worked there, too. We fought over her!

"When she walked in the door, he said, 'Stay away from Margaret. She's mine.'

1. "There's nothing prettier than a 'Beverly Sills' iris," declares Margaret, who likes how the peach-colored flowers look next to her rusty birdbath. She ordered this one from a catalog. "You see those pictures, and you want every iris they have."
2. The highly fragrant *Daphne odora* is a staple in Margaret's winter garden. Some of her daphnes came from *Farmers and Consumers Market Bulletin*, where other gardeners advertise. Margaret has several daphnes planted in various beds next to the tool house and at the entrance to the garden. Her solution for the sometimes finicky plant which will up and die for no reason? "Go get another one immediately."

"We worked out a truce. We arranged for him to go around with her first. He would give me a signal when I could visit with her, and he would leave us alone.

"We learned so much by walking around with her, with that eagle eye of hers for plants. Margaret had started gardening before most of her plants could be bought in this area."

Margaret's Influence on the Popularity of Plants:

By asking a nursery to order a plant she had read about, Margaret was responsible for introducing many new varieties to Atlantans. Her friends joked that before Margaret would finish an article about a new plant, she'd be on the phone with the nursery asking for it.

Margaret never procrastinated where new plants were concerned. There was no holding area at her house. She got right in there, planted things immediately, moved them if they were in the wrong place, and gave them away if they didn't work. There was no hesitation on her part, and her methods gave plants a healthy start and kept the garden beautiful and ever-changing.

However, Margaret admits to a lot of trial and error. As with any garden, things change over the years, especially when you're talking about four decades. Plants disappeared after having been in the garden for years (i.e., a *Daphne odora* would suddenly expire for no reason, or a critter would chew the roots of a prized hosta).

And her emphasis changed. As the garden matured, she found herself increasingly replacing herbaceous plants with shrubs.

"I still have to have my perennials, though. I can't do without my iris and peonies."

3. A bloom on the pineapple lily (*Eucomis* 'Sparkling Burgundy').

4. The appearance of the snow white bells on the native *Halesia diptera* always elicits a phone call from Margaret for everyone to come see. She says the tree is vastly underused in Southern gardens. "It was a stick when I planted it. I haven't had it all that long, though."

5. The flowers of the rare *Michelia maudiae*, which appear in February or March, depending on the weather, closely resemble those of *Magnolia grandiflora*. The shrub—now the height of a tree—was a gift from Margaret's friend Lyndy Broder.

6. *Hosta* 'Sagae', Hosta of the Year 2000.

7. *Hosta* 'Patriot', a gift from Margaret's friend, hosta grower and expert Bud Martin, was the American Hosta Society's Hosta of the Year in 1997.

8. *Hosta* 'White Christmas' always drew gasps from garden visitors.

9. *Rhododendron* 'Roseum Elegans'. Rhododendrons are tricky to grow in the Atlanta area, but this cultivar is more reliable than most. It has lived for thirty years in Margaret's garden. Margaret has another one, *R.* 'Anna Rose Whitney', which is also a good one for the Southeast.

10. *Epimedium sp*. Margaret planted this deciduous groundcover along a grassy path that runs the length of the garden on one side. In back of it are various ferns and hydrangeas, and further down are rows of hostas.

Epimediums bloom in March and April, and, depending on the species, can have flowers of red, pale pink, yellow, or white. The delicate, one-inch flowers resemble the blooms of columbine. When the flowers are finished, thick mounds of heart-shaped leaves emerge for a handsome display the rest of the growing season.

"If you have a shade garden and don't have epimedium, then you're missing out on a very useful plant," says Margaret. "Epimediums look great with hostas and hellebores and ferns and just about anything that grows in the shade."

11. The white form of *Pieris japonica* is planted in several places throughout the garden. It blooms in March with long panicles.

12, 13. The exquisite bud on a "bonus" rose that came with an order of English roses. Margaret is holding the open flower.

Gifts from Friends:

While Margaret combed through local nurseries and scoured mail-order catalogs for interesting finds, many of her plants came from friends or relatives.

"I never bought a hosta," she says. "My friend Bud Martin is a hosta grower, and he gave me every one I ever had. He always grew the latest introductions. I have been so fortunate to know this wonderful man."

When Margaret's garden was on tour or when garden clubs or Master Gardener groups came, you would see the notebooks come out. Margaret knew most of the Latin names of her plants and could tell you the story behind a flower, where she got it, and how it came to be in her garden.

But even though she kept up with what had just come on the market, she took great delight in finding out about something she was unfamiliar with.

"A gardener never gets through learning," she would say. "That's why this is the greatest hobby in the world. There's something new every day. It's so exciting. If I wake up at night, I lie there and landscape and move plants around in my head."

14. A summer bloomer, *Hibiscus syriacus* 'Bluebird', is a form of the old-fashioned Rose of Sharon. Margaret ordered her specimen from Wayside Gardens.

15. A split corona type narcissus. Margaret has added daffodils throughout the years in several of the island beds.

From Margaret's Journal:

February 4, 2003

A warm day (sixty-five degrees) after such a cold January. It's so nice to be out in the garden again. I cut all the old, ugly leaves off the helleborus, and they look so much better. My yard man, Jason, cut off all of the brown foliage on the epimedium with his weed eater.

There are two 'Taylor's Perfection' camellias in full bloom, and the new foliage of the epimedium with the delicate yellow flowers is so pretty as a ground cover for them. This is my favorite ground cover for the shade. It is deciduous and spreads, but it's not invasive and can be divided any time.

16. How *Spiraea* 'Fujino Pink' came to be in Margaret's garden (from Margaret's journal): "When I go to the Southeastern Flower Show, I always enjoy the commercial row to see what I can find that I don't already have. Two years ago, I saw a plant that said 'Pink Spiraea.' Well, I had never heard of a pink spirea, so I brought two of them home. The buds are pink, but the plant is snow white when it is in full bloom—a beautiful spirea. I'm going to plant one next to the pieris for a pretty companion plant. I enjoy grouping plants when they are blooming."

17. *Abelia chinensis* grows along the driveway. This is another plant Margaret feels should be in every garden. She bought hers at a sale sponsored by the Atlanta Botanical Garden where she first saw the hard-to-find plant. In July, the shrub has pinkish-white, fragrant flowers, which are highly attractive to butterflies. In fall, the lilac-shaped flower clusters fade to green and contrast beautifully with *Camellia sasanqua* 'Pink Snow'.

18

19

From Margaret's Journal:

March 27, 2003

A beautiful warm day—seventy-four degrees. I have been in the garden all day. The viburnums are still providing fragrance.

My friend Lyndy Broder came over this afternoon and brought me a plant that I have been wanting for some time—a *Michelia maudiae*, which is a rare form of banana shrub. And what a great plant—already six feet tall.

After we toured the garden, we sat on a bench and had a wonderful time. Lyndy is president of the Georgia Perennial Plant Association, and just last week was the speaker at their meeting on clematis, which is her specialty. I showed her my *Clematis* 'Henryi' full of blooms at the top of a dead tea olive that was killed this winter. She told me to cut the clematis to within six inches of the ground in January.

I know she knows what she's talking about, but I'm so happy to have these blooms up there, I don't know what to do.

March has been a good month for the garden—no severe cold weather and no wind and lots of rain. We were so lucky. I have seen snow in March.

18. The elegant leaves of a toad lily (*Tricyrtis sp.*) have a thin white margin. A special friend brought Margaret this unusual variegated form. The shade plant blooms in autumn.
19. The State Flower of Georgia—the Cherokee rose (*Rosa laevigata*)—blooms in April at the very back of Margaret's garden where the rambling plant has plenty of room. Although it is the state flower (said to have been grown extensively by Cherokee Native-Americans), the plant is actually native to China and Southeast Asia.

20, 21. Orange flowers are not common in Margaret's garden (she likes pinks and purples best), but she grows this pomegranate shrub for its brilliant blooms. "Sandra Jonas brought me this, and people are always asking what these flowers are. This bush does not have fruit, though, just flowers."

" *I like to group plants when they're in bloom.* "

— *Margaret Moseley*

Margaret's Plant Combinations

Part of the beauty of Margaret's garden can be attributed to her sense of how to combine plants by color and texture. Some of her successes, she says, happened by accident. But friends who are garden designers suspect differently. They insist that Margaret has a special vision for how plants should complement one another.

"For someone who claims she didn't know what she was doing, she's done a masterful job," contends Sandra Jonas, a landscape designer who says she has built her garden with Margaret's plants. "It makes me think, why did I spend five years in school for this?"

Margaret says she usually likes to group blooming plants, instead of showcasing just one specimen alone.

Many examples over the years stand out. Margaret planted clear pink *Astilbe* 'Rheinland' next to silvery green *Artemisia* x 'Powis Castle'. Coming up between the two plants was the waist-high, velvety purple Japanese iris, *Iris ensata* 'Summer Storm'. Margaret also liked to use 'Powis Castle' with a favorite pink daylily, *Hemerocallis* 'Lullabye Baby'.

1. At the back of the garden, Margaret planted a hybrid yellow native azalea ("It's fragrant," she says) to reflect the leaf color of *Spiraea* x *bumalda* 'Goldflame'. She recommends this particular mounding type spirea for its heat tolerance.
2. Margaret suspended a hanging basket of pink petunias to echo the color of blooms on *Rhododendron* 'Roseum Elegans' seen in the background.

Another memorable combination at the back of her garden consisted of a tall yellow Exbury azalea underplanted with a row of deep blue dwarf iris.

Close to one of the stone benches is a composition that depends on texture and foliage. A large clump of *Hosta* 'Blue Angel' is surrounded by maidenhair fern. The giant ribbed, blue-tinted leaves in the midst of the delicate green foliage and black stems of the fern create a stunning contrast.

Probably her most outstanding winter accomplishment—at its best during the month of February—was a *Daphne odora*, which had muted pink-mauve flowers, planted amid a generous clump of Lenten rose, *Helleborus* x *hybridus* (formerly *H. orientalis*) with very dark, dusky maroon blossoms.

3. Purple smoketree (*Cotinus coggygria* 'Royal Purple') and a fragrant yellow native azalea make for an interesting contrast.
4. *Hosta* 'Sagae', a gift from Margaret's hosta-grower friend Bud Martin, is in the company of a lilac-colored hydrangea.

5. Margaret loves pinks and purples, and even though she has many other colors throughout the garden, it's this combination she loves best. A pinkish version of the native *Phlox divaricata* has been left to naturalize around the bold leaves of *Eucomis* 'Sparkling Burgundy'. A pink astilbe is just beginning to show buds.

6. Margaret planted the purple *Clematis* 'Jackmanii' to wind through a purple smoketree (*Cotinus coggygria* 'Royal Purple'). The two hues make a startling, but beautiful contrast.

7. Golden daylilies with ruffled edges stand out against an oakleaf hydrangea.

8. Near her back porch, Margaret planted a combination at its best in May. A late-blooming pink gumpo azalea is contrasted with variegated hostas. A blue lacecap hydrangea is just starting to bloom.

9. Next to the carport, a planter overflows with a sedum in bloom. Set in the middle is a dark evergreen conifer. A hosta juts up informally. The green palm-like leaves of hellebores planted in the ground provide yet another leaf size and texture.

10. Along the driveway, the bold clusters of *Abelia chinensis* in its autumnal green stage make an unlikely complement to *Camellia sasanqua* 'Pink Snow'. The coarse texture of what Margaret refers to as "an abelia everybody ought to have" is effective next to the dark, glossy foliage of the sasanqua.

"*I think I can name every friend I have just by looking out there.*"

— Margaret Moseley,
Southern Living *magazine*, May 2000

Passalong & Heirloom Plants

When you leave Margaret's garden with a plant, you leave with some good advice and a story attached to it.

— Tara Dillard

A journalist once called Margaret the original Passalong Lady, meaning that she shared plants—especially old-fashioned Southern favorites and heirloom varieties—with others. Many of the plants in the garden were given to her by friends and relatives who had, in turn, obtained bulbs or cuttings from long-deceased relatives or from old homesteads.

The Story of the Pink Mystery Rose

This is one of those "near-miss" stories.

In the early 1970s, Margaret was visiting her aunt in Veazey, Georgia, in Greene County. The aunt told Margaret she needed to propagate a very fragrant and beautiful pink rose that had belonged to her grandmother, Lula Channell. No one knew where Lula had obtained the rose, whether it had been a gift or if it had been a passalong plant from a neighbor or friend. Margaret's aunt estimated the one plant had been there for well over 100 years.

1. Margaret's grandmother's rose. The fragrant flower has never been identified.
2. All of Margaret's peonies came from a friend who sold her house and moved into an apartment. "She asked if I'd like to have her peonies, and I said I would. I dug all of them up and brought them to my garden."

3. Margaret's grandmother's rose in full flower.
4. A photograph taken in 1907 in Greene County, Georgia, shows Margaret's grandmother, Lula Channell (seated, holding baby), Margaret's mother, Mary Carolyn ("Carrie") at age eleven (standing, back row, second from right), and Margaret's great-grandmother standing in the second row. It was Lula Channell who planted the rose that thrives in Margaret's garden. Margaret's great-grandfather, Thomas Jefferson "Fox" Marchman, took the photograph. "Uncle Fox," as he was known around Greene County, survived the Battle of Gettysburg in early July 1863, but was shot in the leg on June 1, 1864, at Cold Harbor, Virginia. However, he stayed until the end of the war and was present when Gen. Robert E. Lee surrendered at Appomattox, Virginia, on April 9, 1865.

That September, Margaret went back and made a cutting from the rose and took it home. She stuck the piece in the ground next to an outside faucet and forgot all about it.

The next spring, Margaret looked down, and on the eight-inch-high "stick" was a bud. "I never will forget walking out there. That bud was the tiniest thing you've ever seen, but it was going to bloom, right out here by the spigot. That's where it all started. You talk about getting excited. I couldn't believe that tiny little stem had lived."

From that one piece, Margaret has rooted hundreds and given them away. The shrub blooms from late April until the first frost.

Margaret's friend Jeane Jones, who moved the plant Margaret gave her from Stone Mountain to Alpharetta to Dalton, Georgia, raves about the rose, how it is always full of blooms and has never had any disease or insect problems. When Jeane had a double knee replacement, her daughter brought her a big bouquet of the roses.

So, what is this rose? Margaret says two men who were rosarians came to her garden on a hydrangea tour one year. They were fascinated with the flower, but couldn't identify it. Because of its characteristics—long stems, pointed buds, fragrance, great for cutting, and a long blooming season—Margaret believes it is some kind of tea rose.

"I've rooted worlds of them," she says. "Everyone who has it loves it. We just don't know what the name of it is."

Poppies—Like the Loaves and the Fishes

Margaret gives this account of how her fifty-by-sixty-foot poppy patch came to be:

"The poppies blooming at the back of the garden came from just one original plant.

"When I was twelve years old, my next door neighbor sold bunches of poppies for 35 cents. After we moved to this house, I brought her out here. She was so happy I was going to have a garden. She must have been ninety then. I got one poppy plant out of her garden. It's hard to transplant a poppy, and I didn't think it would live, but it did. Now there are thousands of plants of different colors. Some are single; others are shaggy and very double. All of them came from that one poppy plant."

For years, Margaret collected seeds from poppies and reseeding impatiens and sold them in the *Farmers and Consumers Market Bulletin*, published by the Georgia Department of Agriculture. Like her mentor, garden writer Elizabeth Lawrence, Margaret corresponded with the people who bought her seeds. The book, *Gardening for Love*, edited by Allen Lacy (Duke University Press), is Elizabeth Lawrence's account of her own correspondence with readers of market bulletins in several states.

5. Margaret's poppy patch.
6. White dwarf flowering almond (*Prunus glandulosa* 'Alba'). Margaret's mother gave her both the pink and white forms of this old-fashioned shrub. The double flowers literally cover the three- to four-foot-high upright branches in spring. Thomas Jefferson grew dwarf flowering almond at Monticello. The plant is seldom offered in garden centers, but it is often seen in yards in the rural South. Branches can be cut in winter and forced into flower in a vase placed in a warm, sunny spot in the house.

7. Hardy gladiolus (*Gladiolus sp.*). Margaret figures this hardy gladiolus is at least 150 years old. "My cousins gave me the bulbs, which had come from their grandmother. She died in 1932 at the age of ninety-six," says Margaret. "They called it Jacob's Ladder because of the way the flowers opened up the stem." The bulbs still come up around an old homestead in Henry County, Georgia.

8. St. Joseph's Lily (*Hippeastrum* x *johnsonii*). This hardiest of all amaryllis came from a friend who Margaret says eventually died of cancer. "I remember he brought it to me on a garbage can lid," says Margaret. "It's lived in this same spot for forty years."

It is believed that the bulbs of *H.* x *johnsonii* arrived in the United States in the mid-1800s from England, where it was a chance hybrid in the garden of a watchmaker named Johnson, around 1800. St. Joseph's Lily multiplies rapidly, and the bulbs are often found in old gardens and cemeteries across the Southeast. The flowers are at their peak in the month of May around Atlanta.

9. Pearlbush (*Exochorda racemosa*). This is an old-fashioned plant Margaret found on the back of the property when she moved there in 1965. In March, buds in the shape of round "pearls" open to pure white blooms. While this was long considered a passalong plant, the shrubs, which can grow as high as fifteen feet, can, on occasion, be found in nurseries.

10. *Paeonia* 'Festiva Maxima' is white with red splotches. "In the 1960s, I won a silver plate from Rich's department store's flower show with a bloom of 'Festiva Maxima'," recalls Margaret. This heirloom peony dates from the 1850s. It is one of the best peonies for the southeastern United States.

11. Parrot Lily (*Alstroemeria pulchella*). The common garden variety of alstroemeria has red, tube-shaped whirls of flowers tipped in green, rising on single stems from basal foliage. Native to South America, this is one passalong plant (rarely do you see it offered in nurseries) Margaret wishes she'd never seen. The small bulbils multiply readily and can take over a flower bed in a season. Margaret has given many clumps away, but has not succeeded in eradicating the stubborn plants from her garden. Both the foliage and the flowers are highly attractive to deer.

12. Spring Starflower (*Ipheion uniflorum*). Margaret believes that ipheion was brought into her garden when someone gave her another type of plant. The bulbs have spread to form a carpet in spring. Margaret has the white flowering form (blue is more common). If you pick a flower, it has a sweet scent. If you crush the leaves, they smell like onion. Grow the white or blue form under a weeping cherry tree or to edge a path.

13. Reseeding impatiens outline the island beds in summer. For years, Margaret sold impatiens and poppy seeds in the *Farmers and Consumers Market Bulletin*, published by the Georgia Department of Agriculture. Margaret enjoyed corresponding with gardeners who purchased her seeds.

14. Mariana Maiden Fern (*Thelypteris torresiana*). The Mariana maiden fern pops up everywhere in Margaret's garden. Years ago, Margaret planted a single specimen in her garden. She liked the fact that the fern grew almost waist high and lent a light and airy tropical look to shady areas. The next thing she knew, though, her garden was beginning to look like the jungle floor. Ferns were popping up in places where they weren't invited, and she had a new force to reckon with.

Margaret was hardly dissatisfied, however. She allowed the fern to filter up through hydrangeas, making for a pleasing combination. The fern also turned out to be a complement to other plants. A slide I took once shows a single flower of the beautiful daylily 'Shady Lady' (light yellow with a dark maroon eye) encased in a frothy surround of green Mariana maiden fern. It almost looked like a flower arrangement.

"I love it," Margaret says. "I give a lot of it away. It does spread, but it's not a nuisance. If it comes up where I don't want it, I just take the scissors and snip it off."

15. Money Plant (*Lunaria annua*). Margaret has both the purple and white flowering forms of lunaria. The variegated plant seen here came from California. While I was walking through a garden in Marin County, I saw a single plant with a white flower and didn't recognize it because of the unusual leaves. I later asked the gardener for seeds and gave some to Margaret. The first year, the biennial produces thick basal leaves. The second year, the plant flowers and then produces the "coins" containing seeds. The leaves make a great show in a shady part of the garden. Lunaria is best passed along as seeds, as it is difficult to transplant.

16. The white flowering version of *Lunaria annua* has been reseeding in Margaret's garden for over fifteen years. To get started with money plant, sow seeds in fall in a shady location. The next spring, leaves will emerge, but no flowers. The following fall, sow more seeds. You'll be assured of two consecutive years of flowers, since this is a biennial plant. After the second year, the plants should reseed.

17. Hydrangeas have always been a passalong plant, since they are easily propagated by layering.

18. Margaret still has daylilies that have been in her garden for forty years. This one was a gift from a hybridizer friend.

"*Oh my goodness. I have met the most wonderful friends in the world because of my garden. That just about says it all.*"

— *Margaret Moseley*

Friends

Margaret has influenced and inspired a generation of gardeners by welcoming people to her garden, answering questions, giving away plants, and by sharing her experiences and successes and failures.

You'd go to Margaret's garden, and, on the way home, your heart would be beating fast with ideas you'd gleaned—plants you wanted to try, combinations you hadn't thought of, and always, a renewed desire to garden. Most likely, you had something Margaret had dug and given you in a plastic grocery bag. Several wonderful gardens exist now, all because of Margaret.

Lyndy Broder, who served as vice-president of the International Clematis Society and travels all over the world to visit gardens and clematis hybridizers, credits Margaret for the inspiration behind her own multi-acre garden. Lyndy is past president of the Georgia Perennial Plant Association and a member of several plant societies. Her garden, which includes hundreds of varieties of clematis,

1. Penny McHenry, founder of the American Hydrangea Society, and Margaret were best friends and shared many plants.
2. Margaret introduced *Camellia* x 'Fragrant Pink' to many gardeners. She bought several plants as gifts to friends. Jeane Jones has used the flowers for winter centerpieces.

3. Lyndy Broder with a bouquet of azaleas in Margaret's front yard.
4. Margaret encouraged many visitors and friends to plant *Hydrangea arborescens* 'Annabelle'.

has appeared in articles in *Southern Living* magazine and the *Atlanta Journal-Constitution* and was the subject of an episode of *A Gardener's Diary* on Home & Garden Television.

From a Recollection by Lyndy Broder:

As a young newlywed, my husband took me to visit one of his bank customers in Decatur. All I remember about that day was the most glorious blue hydrangeas and a wistful longing to recreate that loveliness myself. My life was full of raising four busy children and pursuing a challenging career.

Fast forward twenty-five years…After taking an early retirement, my first action was to sign up for the Master Gardener course. My second was to join the American Hydrangea Society. I eagerly anticipated my first hydrangea tour in June of 1998. As I walked into this Decatur garden, *déjà vu* overcame me. The joyfulness of those blue hydrangeas from so many years past was as powerful as my first encounter.

I lingered in the garden, traversing its many paths several times, eagerly waiting for the garden owner to be free from her many admirers. I tentatively approached Margaret, still not sure if this was in fact the same garden I had visited twenty-five years before. As I asked my gardening questions, I wove into the conversation that I had come from Stockbridge—the connection was made, and I was the one monopolizing her attention while other garden visitors circled around us, waiting for the chance to ask Margaret a myriad of garden questions.

At that second meeting, Margaret became my gardening mentor. Although I was finally becoming a gardener in my retirement, I never envisioned that it was possible to create a garden at the age of fifty. I had thought it was much too late to be planting trees and shrubs and live long enough to realize their beauty. Margaret, herself, began serious gardening at fifty-two, after she had raised her own four children and helped with grandchildren. She had created a treasure to be envied by many. It was her inspiration that allowed me to see what I could also accomplish. It wasn't too late.

Over the years, Margaret was a constant instructor on gardening techniques, but more importantly, a sense of design. She is a hands-on gardener who intimately understands each plant in relationship with other plants—the sunshine, airflow, focal points. To garden in Margaret's style, you must exist in your garden, total symbiosis. It entails intimate knowledge and close encounters of every aspect of your garden.

Because of Margaret's influence, my garden is so much more than it would have been. When I had the opportunity to be in a small article in *Southern Living* magazine, Margaret laughingly told me that she was "accustomed to being on the cover."

Margaret Moseley is justifiably the quintessential "Gardening Cover Girl."

When Margaret turned ninety, Jeane Jones, wife of Margaret's Presbyterian minister, wrote what she called an "Ode to Margaret." She also included an extensive list of plants in her garden that had come directly from Margaret:

Musings about Margaret on her Ninetieth Birthday

Nearly everything I have in my garden came from Margaret Moseley's garden or was her recommendation. This is so much the case that I refer to mine as "Margaret's North." And many things that didn't come directly from her came from her friends' gardens where she would take me to visit.

With my fledgling efforts at trying to garden, it was personally hard to impress Margaret, THE garden diva with decades of experience. Once, when she was in my garden and had had a brief stroll, I was thrilled to hear her say, "You've got two things I want." *What could it be?* My mind raced. *Did I have even one new plant introduction that had somehow escaped her purchase?*

"That trellis and that potting shed," she quickly quipped.

The walls of Margaret's sunroom are plastered in pictures of her garden, which has appeared in *Southern Living*, *Better Homes and Gardens*, *Atlanta Magazine*, *Atlanta Homes and Lifestyles* magazine, and often the *Atlanta Journal-Constitution's* Home & Garden section. Several local organizations have honored her within the last year for being such an inspiration in the gardening community. Recent "field trips" to Massee Lane Camellia Gardens, Ashe-Simpson, and Land Arts nurseries were not just buying trips with her, but another opportunity to see how often she is recognized and admired in the larger world of gardening.

It is her combination of knowledge, wit, and wisdom and her generosity that makes devotees of all who cross her path—or better still, walk with her in her garden. It is in honor of her ninetieth birthday, May 28, 2006, that I offer the following:

Things I have learned about gardening from Margaret——thus far

– Take a sack lunch with you when you're going out of town to a nursery. Don't waste time on food.

– If you're over fifty-five, buy a plant in the biggest size container they have. You don't have time to wait for it to mature.

– You can transplant anything almost anytime—if you can keep it watered.

– Every garden needs a bluebird house. Put it where you can see it.

5. Friends gather every May 28 for Margaret's birthday. Jeane Jones says she has an entire garden full of plants from Margaret.

– A garden keeps you going. "What would I do without my garden?" she says.

– Limb up shrubs so that you have more room to plant underneath.

– Every plant that doesn't live is an opportunity to try something new.

– Get rid of anything that is just taking up space.

– And, above all else, know when to show restraint. Remember the quote "Once I had a lovely garden, and I ruined it with plants."

                With love,
                Jeane

The following are plants Margaret shared with me straight from her garden and into a plastic grocery bag. She used to have a plaque in one of her beds that read: "Your feet are killing me." Therefore, she did most of the digging, though she would allow me to fetch the shovel from her potting shed and the bags from her laundry room:

6. One of many types of ferns in Margaret's garden, Japanese painted fern (*Athyrium niponicum* var. *pictum*), has blue-gray fronds. Seen here with blue columbine, which has seeded in the long border.

Japanese painted fern (*Athyrium niponicum* var. *pictum*)
Maidenhair fern (*Adiantum capillus-veneris*)
Peacock fern (*Selaginella uncinata*)
Arbovitae fern (*Selaginella braunii*)
Mariana maiden fern (*Thelypteris torresiana*)
Variegated Japanese knotweed; fleece flower (*Fallopia japonica* 'Variegata')
Variegated liriope (*Liriope muscari* 'Variegata'). This came and remains with oxalis in it.
Black mondo (*Ophiopogon planiscapus* 'Nigrescens')
Archangel—Silver beacon ground cover (*Lamium maculatum* 'Beacon Silver')
Stonecrop (*Sedum sieboldii*)
Parrot lily (*Alstroemeria pulchella*)
Hardy begonia (*Begonia grandis*)
Purple loosestrife (*Lythrum salicaria*)
Hardy terrestrial orchid (*Bletilla striata*)
Hardy plumbago (*Ceratostigma plumbaginoides*)
Lenten rose (*Helleborus* x *hybridus*—formerly *Helleborus orientalis*)
Fairy wings (*Epimedium* x *versicolor* 'Sulphureum')
Japanese aster (*Kalimeris pinnatifida* 'Hortensis')
Lamb's ear (*Stachys byzantina*)
Wormwood (*Artemisia* x 'Powis Castle')
Stokes' aster (*Stokesia laevis*)
Wild geranium (*Geranium maculatum*)
Golden creeping Jenny (*Lysimachia nummularia* 'Aurea')
Poppy seed (*Papaver somniferum* var. *paeoniflorum*)
Iris (*Iris germanica*)
Pink daylily (*Hemerocallis* 'Lullaby Baby')

7. All of Margaret's bearded irises have been given to her. In turn, she's shared them with friends.
8. Arborvitae fern (*Selaginella braunii*) is an excellent texture plant and a good ground cover for the woodland garden. The foliage looks like cedar.

Cuttings: These I Rooted, and They are in My Garden Today:

Double oakleaf hydrangea (*Hydrangea quercifolia* 'Snowflake')
Her grandmother's purple hydrangea (*Hydrangea macrophylla* unknown)
Her grandmother's rose—rooted and shared with other friends of mine (*Rosa* unknown)
Cape jasmine—the cemetery one (*Gardenia jasminoides* unknown)
Double pink althea (*Hibiscus syriacus*)
Montbretia (*Crocosmia sp.*)

Gift Shrubs from Margaret:

Lacecap hydrangea (*Hydrangea serrata* 'Blue Billow')—a shoot dug by Walter when he went to get her to visit my garden in about 2006.
Royal Standard hosta (*Hosta* x 'Royal Standard')
Grancy graybeard (*Chionanthus virginicus*)
Camellia (*Camellia japonica* 'Magnoliaeflora')
Hybrid camellia (*Camellia* x 'Fragrant Pink')
Camellia (*Camellia japonica* 'White Empress')

9. Lamb's ear (*Stachys byzantina*) is a good ground cover for sun and easy to divide.
10. Margaret has shared hundreds of Lenten roses (*Helleborus* x *hybridus*, formerly *H. orientalis*) with friends.

Things She Told Me to Buy: "If you see it, buy it."

Flowering apricot (*Prunus mume*)
Bigleaf hydrangea (*Hydrangea macrophylla* 'Pia')
Hybrid hydrangea (*Hydrangea serrata* x 'Preziosa')
Antique rose (*Rosa* 'Mutabilis')
Chinese snowball (*Viburnum macrocephalum*)
Fragrant viburnum (*Viburnum* x *carlcephalum*)
Korean spice viburnum (*Viburnum carlesii*)
Fragrant daphne (*Daphne odora*)
Purple pineapple lily (*Eucomis* 'Sparkling Burgundy')
Climbing hydrangea (*Schizophragma hydrangeoides* 'Moonlight')
Snowbell tree (*Styrax japonicus*)
Smooth hydrangea (*Hydrangea arborescens* 'Annabelle')
Plum yew (*Cephalotaxus harringtonia*)

Hostas—That was one thing Margaret didn't divide, and most of hers were handsome and huge. I guess that's why.

11. Margaret has shared poppy seeds, which originally came from one plant, with many friends. The seeds should be planted on bare ground in the fall.

12. One of the many hydrangeas given to Margaret by friends.

From Gloria Ward, President of the American Hydrangea Society:

Margaret has been such a wonderful inspiration to me. Knowing that she created all the beauty in her garden after she turned fifty years old gives me hope and inspiration. Her enthusiasm about her garden, marveling over whatever is in bloom at the time, is so precious.

Margaret gave me my first hellebores and epimediums. Her enthusiasm regarding camellias and gardenias is infectious. Every time I look at one in my garden or any garden, it makes me think of Margaret. I can always hear her "in my head" when she exclaims that her garden "is the prettiest it's ever been!"

Probably my favorite memory of Margaret and her garden was one time while visiting there with several friends, Margaret served her famous almond tea while we sat in the center of her garden admiring all the beauty. Each of us had a fabulous view, no matter which seat we were in. What fun we had that day. She is such an inspiration to us all.

Another time with Margaret, we went to nurseries in search of new and different plants. She loved Land Arts, Jane Bath's nursery, especially because Jane offered *Hydrangea macrophylla* 'Margaret Mosley'. I am so happy I have one in my collection of hydrangeas.

Margaret always wants to share what she has with you. What a generous, loving, wonderful lady. I feel so privileged to know her.

13. Friends celebrate Margaret's birthday on May 28 every year. Left to right: Phyllis McGuinn, Margaret Moseley, Lyndy Broder, Marsha Yeager, Sandra Jonas.

Fan Mail

Mrs. Margaret Moseley
3254 Wesley Chapel Road
Decatur 30034
Georgia   U.S.A.

July 10, 1996

Dear Mrs Moseley -

I was delighted to get your note with all the answers and the nice packet of impatient seeds. I did precisely what you said - I went to the nursery the next morning and found they had a new shipment of Annabelles. I bought two! One for my garden and one for Mother's. They've bloomed steadily but my blooms are only medium size. Yours were tremendous!

The impatient seeds sprouted quickly - I can't wait to get them going in my garden. With the help of an older friend who has a beautiful English garden - and her pass along plants - my beds are being transformed. I've been studying E.L.'s *A Southern Garden* and Carol Bishop Hipps' *In a Southern Garden* extensively. Your video was so delightful - I keep hoping that they will repeat it again soon - What you have -- is what I want! You certainly imparted a lot of information and beauty - during that stroll through your garden.

Thank you again for the seeds and the good information - consider me "under your wing."

Affectionately,
Melissa

Melissa Mahone
7802 Haven St SE
Huntsville AL

May 5, 1997

Dear Mrs. Moseley,

I saw your most beautiful garden on the Gardeners Diary with Erica Glasner and wrote to HGTV to inquire if you had given Erica Glasner your almond tea recipe.

Would it be possible for you to send me your recipe for your almond tea? also could you send me one of your poppy and impatient seeds? I think you mentioned on TV. that they were $1.00 a piece. I'm enclosing $3.00 and extra postage so you could send them.

You had so many beautiful flowers in your garden and I wish I could grow some of them but I live in a zone 5 so it would be impossible.

I think its wonderful that you want to garden until you are 99 years old. Gardening can keep you healthy.

I will be most anxiously awaiting your reply.

Mrs. Sharon Campione
4820 Lyell Road
Spencerport, New York

Envelope (front):

AIR MAIL

Mrs Margaret Mosely
3254 We...
Decatu...
U...

[Stamps: 3 × 45c Australia]

Letter from Australia:

The Garden of Arcadia
1-21 Nichols Road
Narbethong 3778
Victoria
Australia.

Dear Margaret Moseley

Having viewed a complete ½ hr video of you in your gorgeous garden on cable television, I had to write & tell you how very enjoyable it was. Day lillies & huge hydrangeas "Stunning". We also have a passion for gardening & recently have opened our 5 acre country garden to the public & will be included in the Australian Open Garden Scheme April 99. I am enclosing 2 photos, maybe you will get some idea of how we spend our time, money and energy, but never fail to be enthused by a beautiful garden & spend hours in the evenings looking & reading about lovely gardens such as yours. I am planning on planting lots of daylillies

---

Letter from Mitzi W. Thornell:

Mitzi W. Thornell
449 Dry Creek Road
Waynesboro, TN 38485

19 February 1998

Margaret Moseley
3254 Wesley Chapel Rd.
Atlanta, GA 30034

Dear Margaret,

I enjoyed very much the stroll through your garden and visiting with you ta... gardening. A Gardener's Diary is my favorite TV program and I enjoy all ... but I have never written to anyone about one of them. It just seems that y... I have known and visited with before. I surely wish we could sit down in t... glass of almond iced tea and just talk gardening.

I am very interested in the address of the Farmer's and Consumer's Market... inclosing a SASE for your reply and do so very much appreciate your trou... would love a copy of the almond tea recipe. Sounds wonderful.

Thank you for your help.

Mitzi W. Thornell

Mitzi W Thornell

Letter from Melissa Mahone:

Your garden was so beautiful. I'm striving for "that look" but have a way to go yet. I really enjoyed your discussion of the plants.

I know you're busy at this time of year — but would love to have your help!

Are the hydrangeas that you cut back each March the "French" hydrangeas — blue, pink — based on soil acidity? The size of your blooms were fantastic! I thought this hydrangea bloomed on old growth — but I want to do whatever you are doing!

I would love to purchase the poppy and impatient seeds from you. Do you have any of the taller impatients? They're hard to find in the nurseries. Do you sell plants of the Marianna climbing fern?

Sincerely,
Melissa Mahone
7802 Haven Street SE
Huntsville, AL 35802
(505) 883-5980 after 7pm CST

"Southern Illuminations"
306 Government St.
Wetumpka, AL 36092

"Herbals" designed by
Carol Barksdale

Letter from June 2, 1996:

June 2, 1996

Dear Mrs Moseley,

I recently was delighted to see you and your gardens on Home & Garden TV. I was listening and looking so hard — I forgot to write down all the details! I hope you can help me with some of my questions.

Is it Elizabeth Lester (?) that authored the books on southern gardens?

How does one subscribe to the Farmers & Gardeners' Market bulletin?

"*I snapped off a piece and hid it in my pocketbook.*"

— Margaret Moseley

Margaret-isms

If nothing else, Margaret kept us all entertained with her garden stories.

The Cemetery Gardenia

One of my favorite stories from Margaret's vast repertoire concerns a special gardenia. Many years ago, Margaret was attending a funeral in a cemetery at a Methodist church out in the country.

The grieving family was sitting under the tent, listening to the minister's words about their loved one. Standing behind them was Margaret. Her heart was pounding, but not because of the scene directly in front of her. It was because she had spied a gardenia in bloom on the other side of the cemetery.

All she could think about during the reading of the Twenty-Third Psalm was getting a cutting of that gardenia. She figured that if it was blooming away in this cemetery in the blazing sun, that it must be very hardy.

1. Ginkgo leaves after "The Fall."
2. One of many lacecap hydrangeas in Margaret's garden.

3. The Cemetery Gardenia today. People from as far away as California have a plant from Margaret's one stolen cutting.
4. A bloom from the Cemetery Gardenia, which is now twelve feet tall.
5. Margaret would bake cornbread for the bluebirds. She insisted the mother and father never minded when she removed the nest to show off the eggs.
6. The moment before the baby bluebird flew. Margaret got to see it after all.

Finally, the graveside service was over, and she made a beeline for the plant.

"I snapped off a piece and hid it in my pocketbook," she said. "When I got home I put it in some water, and in no time, it rooted. I have proof that you can have a twelve-foot-tall plant from one twig placed in water."

When asked if she felt any guilt about stealing something at a funeral, she answered, laughing:

"Oh, I think God has forgiven me. I know that because He's let me root hundreds to give away."

April 2

I just checked the nest this year, and there are three beautiful blue eggs. Oh, the joy of living, loving, and gardening. What else can be so beautiful?

Margaret and the Bluebirds

One year, I saw Jeff Potter at the Southeastern Flower Show, and he asked me how my garden was, and I told him it would look good if I didn't have so many weeds.

Several weeks later, on a beautiful Saturday morning, he drove up, and I said, "Jeff, what are you doing here today?" He said he had come to pull weeds for me. What a kind friend. When he was way in the back where the vegetable garden used to be, he saw my old bluebird house. He told me he was going to bring it down near the sunroom so I could enjoy the birds. I told him I didn't think they would come that close to the house. He said, "We'll see."

Within two hours, before he got through weeding, the birds were on top of that house. I had not seen a bluebird in years. They have come back every year, and what a joy they have been.

The house is about ten feet from my sunroom, and I sit out there and watch them feed their babies. Last year there were four babies. I sometimes bake cornbread for them, and they love it.

A Baby Flies

One mid-July day, I was out visiting Margaret. We were walking around the garden, and I noticed she was acting very distracted and not paying attention to what I was saying.

Finally, she told me what was wrong. This was the day she thought the newest crop of baby bluebirds would fledge. In fact, she said, it could happen any minute, and she didn't want to miss seeing them flying out of the nest.

So, we walked over and were standing right by the box, when all of a sudden a head poked out. I put my camera up and caught the baby just as it was halfway out of the hole, and then it flew out and was gone.

Margaret finally confessed to me that she had secretly wished I wouldn't come that day, as she was afraid she'd miss out on the event. In the end, she was happy I had caught the action.

— *Martha Tate*

The Day the Ginkgo Leaves Fell

It's late November, and Margaret is ninety-five years old:

Margaret has dug in for the duration, and nothing can pry her away from home for the near future.

"Everybody who knows me knows I will not leave home this time of year until the ginkgo leaves have fallen. I'm not going anywhere, even to get my hair fixed."

Margaret planted a ginkgo tree right outside her large sunporch around thirty years ago. "It was about the size of a broom handle, about three feet tall," she recalls. "It's now over forty feet high. My friend Si says they are slow growing, but mine just took off."

Every November, the leaves turn a bright golden yellow, and then all at once, within an hour's time, the silky fans fall to the ground.

"It starts with just one leaf coming down," Margaret explains. "And then, there will be three, and that's when I know they are all about to fall. If you see that one leaf, you'd better find a comfortable chair because you're about to see a show. One of my daughters happened to be over here one year when the leaves started falling. She went out there and stood while they just rained down on her. She couldn't believe it."

Once, a pine tree crashed down in Margaret's yard, taking out one side of the ginkgo.

"Everybody in Atlanta knew it, because I called them up and told them about it. I cried for days. But now, you can't even tell it ever happened."

One November, as I was driving around, I noticed the ginkgo trees around town had turned yellow. I called Margaret to check on the progress, because the night before it had rained and the day was gray and windy and cold.

"Oh, but the leaves make it look like the sun is shining out there. If you stand under it, you can't believe how bright it is overhead," she told me. "It's the prettiest thing you've ever seen."

○·······································○

Another year, I called Margaret because the leaves were late turning.

"My daughter has invited me to Thanksgiving at her house, and I've already warned her. If the ginkgo leaves haven't fallen, I'm not coming. I wait a whole year to watch this happen, and I'm not going to take a chance. I'll just stay here and eat a peanut butter sandwich."

Fortunately, the leaves fell two days before Thanksgiving. It was a close call, but Margaret got to have dinner with family after all.

7. *Ginkgo biloba* at the entrance to Margaret's garden. It was the size of a broomstick when Margaret planted it decades ago.
8. At long last, the fallen leaves.
9. Ginkgo leaves blanket the ground in late November. A cutleaf Japanese maple glows red near the garden pond.

The Sassafras Tree

(From Margaret's Journal):

There are two red 'Governor Mouton' camellias, and I know they must be thirty years old. They are loaded with blooms. For several years, a tree kept coming up in one of them, and I kept cutting it down. About five years ago, I was out there to cut it down again, and my friends Si and Kim Elliott from McDonough stopped by, and Si saw what I was going to cut down. He shamed me for not knowing a sassafras tree and told me not to cut it down. It is a native tree with pale yellow blooms. It is now about fifteen feet tall and five feet above the red camellia. Yes, red and yellow can be pretty together sometimes. The foliage is spectacular in the fall. I am so glad they came by when they did. Sassafras is very difficult to transplant, and I'm so lucky to have it.

The Doomed 'Yuletide'

One day, I went out to Margaret's and was showing her pictures I'd taken through the years. Several of the photographs showed *Camellia sasanqua* 'Yuletide', covered with brilliant red blooms with yellow stamens. One was planted in front of a sourwood tree in a raised bed that had originally surrounded a pine tree, which had been taken down.

"Margaret, that's the most beautiful combination with the red fall leaves and the bright red sasanqua," I said.

"Well, it's a good thing you took a picture, because I'm cutting both of them down."

"You can't do that," I protested. "People would kill to have something so beautiful in their garden."

"Well, I'll think about it," was her reply.

The next spring, I was out in the garden, and realized both the sourwood and the 'Yuletide' were gone.

"Margaret, you cut down one of the prettiest sasanquas in your garden," I lamented as we stood there.

"Well, I needed the room, and it was too big to move. Its trunk was just too thick, and it was blocking my view of 'C. M. Wilson' camellia. Besides, I've got another 'Yuletide' that is just as pretty."

Case closed.

10. A sassafras leaf in fall color.
11. Gone, but not forgotten by at least one person: *Camellia sasanqua* 'Yuletide' and a sourwood tree (*Oxydendrum arboreum*).
12. Margaret and the doomed 'Yuletide'. *Photo: Erica Glasener.*

Moving the Michelia maudiae

Margaret had been so thrilled when Lyndy Broder had brought her a *Michelia maudiae*, a rare and beautiful shrub/tree she had long coveted. One day a couple of years later, Lyndy stopped by to see Margaret on her way to a Master Gardeners' convention.

"Margaret, that michelia will never bloom. It's in too much shade," Lyndy told her.

It would be days before anyone came to help, and when Margaret made up her mind to move something, that was it.

"Lyndy hadn't been gone ten minutes when I went and got the shovel and started digging," said Margaret. "The tree was already ten feet tall and was so heavy I had to drag it across to where I wanted it. When I finally got it over there, I just stood it up and put some rocks around it. I never even planted it."

This happened when Margaret was eighty-nine.

"Somehow it rooted, and I bet it's twenty feet tall now. It has the prettiest blooms on it you've ever seen."

Neither height, nor weight, nor age could stop Margaret when she decided a plant must be

13.

13. A *Micheliae maudiae* blossom.
14. Margaret, at ninety-six, sharing stories with *A Gardener's Diary* host Erica Glasener in the sitting area on a late winter day.
15. The lacecap 'Lady in Red' was hybridized by Michael A. Dirr, author of books on woody plants, viburnums, and hydrangeas. Margaret would see a new plant and "have to have it."

14

15

" *If you see a plant you want, buy it right then. Don't wait, or it may be gone when you come back.* "

— *Margaret Moseley*

How to have a successful garden. Advice, tips, hints from Margaret.

As a hands-on gardener for over four decades, Margaret amassed a lot of experience with plants. She has always been willing to pass along any hints that will make gardening more enjoyable and save someone else valuable time and money.

"The first thing I would tell a person is if you dread doing maintenance jobs like weeding and deadheading, don't garden. It should always be a real joy to do whatever needs to be done."

Margaret's List of "Don'ts"

Be careful and don't overdo it. Keep your garden full, but don't overplant. Remember the quote: "Once I had a lovely garden, but I ruined it with plants."

— Don't ever mind moving a plant. Normally, I have to move things four or five times to get them in the right place. I've never thought twice about moving a plant, because I knew where it was going and was excited about its new location.

1. *Hydrangea macrophylla* 'Ayesha' with its unusual spoon-like petals was given to Margaret by a friend. Margaret propagated the plant in order to have one n another part of the garden. She says people rave about the huge, beautiful blooms.
2. Daffodils are planted in many of the island beds around the garden. The foliage should be left to ripen. Cutting or tying up the green foliage will rob the bulbs of nutrients to produce flowers in the future.

Margaret's List of "Don'ts" (cont.)

– Also, I have no patience in waiting. If I want a plant moved, I do it immediately. As long as you can water, you should never fear moving a plant. I don't think I ever lost any plants this way. It's better to get them in a place where they'll have the right amount of sun or shade.

– Don't plant anything with big roots next to the house. Also, remember that camellias, sasanquas, and hollies get very tall. They're not good foundation plants. Plant them where they won't have to be pruned so hard, or at all.

– Don't plant wisteria. Enjoy them along the highway. I've known too many people whose lives were made miserable by Chinese wisteria once it got loose.

– If you see a plant you want, buy it right then. Don't wait, or it may be gone when you come back.

– Never plant a pine tree. They're too brittle and messy.

– Advice from Elizabeth Lawrence: She said not to mulch too much, because mulch encourages voles. I now use pine straw to neaten up the beds, but I've never been a heavy mulcher.

– Plant a lot of daffodils, but plant them in spots where you can allow the foliage to ripen. Don't ever remove the foliage until it turns yellow. I've had so many people ask me why daffodils don't bloom again. Chances are, they ran over the green leaves with a lawn mower.

– Watch out for invasive plants, and don't introduce them to your garden. I thought I'd never get rid of houttuynia. I've had the same problem with alstroemeria. It will take over a bed. I had to get rid of 'Goldheart' English ivy because it started climbing everything in sight.

Dos:

— I like to group plants that bloom at the same time. That will make your garden more beautiful and interesting.

— Know when to get rid of plants. When I receive plants from friends, I'll often give something away to make room. You have to be disciplined and learn to do that.

— Deadhead regularly. I never get through.

— Collect seeds and share them with friends. I'm not a good seed planter, but I'll gladly collect seeds from poppies and larkspur to share with others.

—Take time to grieve for a beloved tree, but try to look at the new opportunities. I lost several large pine trees in my backyard. It seemed like a tragedy at the time. I picked out some trees and shrubs I had wanted to grow and put them right in.

— Seize an opportunity. I thought I would die when I lost a huge limb off my ginkgo tree. I took advantage of the new area and filled it with blue pansies in winter and golden creeping Jenny and petunias in the summer. This also created enough openness for the bluebird box. I have several families of bluebirds every year.

— If you're starting out, plant a male ginkgo tree.

— Plant dogwoods, especially the kousa dogwood (*Cornus kousa*).

— Flowering apricot (*Prunus mume*) is a must for every garden. It blooms in January and February and is so pretty.

— If you live in an area where gardenias are hardy, plant one every twenty-five feet. I have at least a half-dozen kinds.

3. A view out of Margaret's sunroom with 'Sum and Substance' hostas in the foreground.

4. *Cornus kousa* is one of Margaret's favorite trees. It blooms in May, a month after the native dogwoods.

Propagating Plants:

— Gardenias will root in water and can be transferred directly into the ground.

— Hydrangeas can be easily propagated by layering. Take a lower branch, scratch off some of the green bark, make a slight dent in the soil, and place that part of the branch in the ground. Then secure it with a brick. Leave several inches past the brick. After the roots form, cut the new plant away from the mother plant.

— Azaleas can be layered in the same manner as hydrangeas.

— Gather the seeds of cool season annuals—poppies, bachelor's buttons, and larkspur—in June and plant them in fall in newly prepared ground.

— Many plants, like *Phlox divaricata* and *Arum italicum*, spread readily. Dig and share with friends.

Tried and True Methods:

— Place a good sized rock on top of the soil next to a new plant and water evenly for at least a year. The rock keeps the wind from rocking the roots. This applies for plants three feet or taller. I've always done this, and it works.

— Use fertilizer only as needed. If the plants are big, and they bloom, why feed them? However, I have good soil, so if you don't, add compost and fertilizer. I sometimes put in some 10-10-10 and manure when I plant something new.

— Daylily foliage can look unsightly after the flowers are spent. I cut the foliage back to the ground after they bloom. You'll get a new flush of leaves, and this will also give other perennials a chance to shine.

— In early March, cut both peegee hydrangeas (*Hydrangea paniculata*) and Annabelles (*Hydrangea arborescens* 'Annabelle') back to promote larger blooms. These types of hydrangeas bloom on new wood.

— When someone gives me a plant or when I buy one, I make sure it gets into the ground immediately. There's no holding pen at my house. I find a place, even if I have to dig out into the lawn and expand one of my rock-lined beds.

— If you have burrowing critters that are eating roots, place the plant in a black plastic pot with the bottom cut out and plant in the ground.

How to Learn about Gardening and Plants:

— Read every garden book, magazine, and catalog you can get your hands on. You can benefit from what others have done and avoid mistakes they've made. This is a great way to learn about plants, as well.

— Visit nurseries and garden centers regularly. Ask if they'll order a plant for you if they don't have it in stock.

— To learn about plants and remember them, you have to be in contact with them. The best way to know plants is to work with them in your garden.

— I never had time to go on garden tours, but that's a good way to see plants and combinations you like. You get a lot of ideas from what others are doing. I loved having visitors to my garden. I would often receive letters thanking me for introducing them to a favorite plant. I remember one letter in particular where a young woman from Alabama went home and bought 'Annabelle' hydrangeas for herself and her mother. She had not seen them before.

5. *Phlox divaricata* blooms during April and into May. It has a sweet scent and naturalizes without being invasive. This is a good shade or sun plant to share with other gardeners.
6. "I like to group plants that bloom together." *Iris japonica* and azaleas in the April garden.
7. Daylily foliage and flower stalks can be unsightly after they've bloomed. To make your garden look neater, cut back the foliage of daylilies after the blooms are gone. The leaves will flush out and look attractive, and it won't hurt the plant for next year's flowers.

" Growing old, I've been so blessed by the younger garden friends I've made through the years. I'm never lonely. I can't say enough about what gardening has done for me. I wish everybody could have a garden. "

— Margaret Moseley

Finding Health and Happiness in the Garden

> 11-2-95
>
> Dear Martha,
>   Because of you I'm enjoying my garden so much in my twilight years. Thank you.
>
>   Love,
>   Margaret

Twilight years? Little did Margaret know that when she penned this note at age seventy-nine, she was about to enter the prime of her gardening life. In fact, the next decade would bring national attention through scores of articles written about her in books, magazines, and newspapers. There would be three television episodes featuring her garden. Tour groups would come by the busload, one even arriving from North Carolina unannounced.

1. "Margaret in Her Garden." Portrait by Susan Carter Lee, oil on linen. 32"x40."
2. Lush spring scene in the garden.

This exchange took place when Margaret was eighty years old:

Margaret (walking in the garden with her daughter Carol Harris): When I'm gone, I want you children to come and take anything you want from the garden.

Carol: But, Mother, by that time we'll all be too old to dig!

Seventeen years later, Carol says her prophecy has come true.

3. Margaret at age ninety-two, planting pansies with helpers (L) Mike Weathers and (R) Fidel Rodriguez.
4. Margaret's daughter, Carol Harris.
5. Forty-eight years later: the door to the tool house with the original *Hydrangea macrophylla* 'Margaret Moseley'.

Margaret is convinced that working in her garden has contributed to her good health and well-being, and possibly a long life—ninety-seven years and counting. She says it isn't just the physical work—digging, weeding, hauling rocks, lifting containers of plants, rolling a wheelbarrow along the paths—that has made her so energetic. She thinks it's the anticipation that makes all the difference.

"I still get so excited when I see a bud that I know will be open in a few days. I get up every morning full of energy, and I just can't wait to see what's going on in the garden. There's never a dull moment."

Perhaps most of all, it's the friends she's made through her garden who have kept her so lively and in good spirits.

"Garden people are just different from anyone else. I just love them all. When you garden, people come to you. I'm never lonely in my old age."

> "Gardening is so exciting—watching over plants and waiting for them to bloom. That's what gets you outside. There isn't anything like it. I can't wait to get out there every morning."
>
> — Margaret Moseley

INDEX

A

Abelia chinensis, 29, 84, 93
Adiantum capillus-veneris, 110
Aesculus parviflora, 24
Almond tea, 43, 113
Almond tea recipe, 45
Alstroemeria pulchella, 99, 110, 128
Althea, 111
American Camellia Society Headquarters, 71
American Hemerocallis Society, 17
American Hosta Society, 79
American Hydrangea Society, 62, 113
Angel's trumpet, 27
'Annabelle' hydrangea, 10–11, 22
Antique rose, 112
Appomattox, Virginia, 96
Arbovitae fern, 110
Archangel, 110
Artemisia x 'Powis Castle', 89, 110
Arum italicum, 27, 68, 130
Ashe-Simpson Garden Center, 108
Astilbe 'Rheinland', 89
Athyrium niponicum var. *pictum*, 109
Atlanta Botanical Garden, 84
Atlanta Homes and Lifestyles, 10, 12, 42, 108
Atlanta Journal-Constitution, 9, 11–13, 53–54, 106, 108
Atlanta Magazine, 10, 108
Azalea, 18, 23-24, 130-131
'Azure Blue' pansies, 68

B

Bachelor's buttons, 130
Banana shrub, 85
Baptisia, 23
Baptisia alba, 32
Bath, Jane, 113
Battle of Gettysburg, 96
Bearded iris, 22, 36
Beautybush, 22
Begonia grandis, 17, 19, 110
Bender, Steve, 11
Better Homes and Gardens special national edition, 10, 108
Black mondo grass, 110
Bletilla striata, 110
'Bluebird' *althea*, 22
Bluebirds, 118–119
Bottlebrush buckeye, 24
Boxwood, 22
Broder, Lyndy, 79, 85, 105–106, 113, 124
Brugmansia sp., 27
Buddleia davidii, 29

'Butterfly' Japanese maple, 25

C

Camellia, 18, 23–24, 27, 44, 54–55, 61, 113, 128
Camellia japonica, 26, 47
Camellia japonica 'Berenice Boddy', 47
Camellia japonica 'C. M. Wilson', 25, 46–47, 71, 123
Camellia japonica 'Daikagura', 68–69
Camellia japonica 'Debutante', 68
Camellia japonica 'Governor Mouton', 25, 41, 69, 74–75
Camellia japonica 'James Hyde Porter', 75
Camellia japonica 'Lady Clare' ('Empress'), 23, 33, 50, 68, 71–72
Camellia japonica 'Magnoliaeflora' ('Hagoromo', 'Rose of Dawn','Cho-No-Hagasan'), 70, 111
Camellia japonica 'Miss Bessie Beville', 71
Camellia japonica 'Professor Charles S. Sargent', 68
Camellia japonica 'White By the Gate', 27, 70–71
Camellia japonica 'White Empress', 68, 70, 72, 111
Camellia lutchuensis, 69
Camellia sasanqua, 22, 25, 47
Camellia sasanqua 'Cleopatra', 54
Camellia sasanqua 'Cotton Candy', 54–55, 60
Camellia sasanqua 'Jean May', 54–55
Camellia sasanqua 'Kanjiro', 68
Camellia sasanqua 'Leslie Ann', 54–57
Camellia sasanqua 'Martha's Dream', 55, 57–58
Camellia sasanqua 'Mine-No-Yuki' ('Snow', 'White Doves'), 54, 56–57
Camellia sasanqua 'Pink Snow', 27, 54, 56, 84, 93
Camellia sasanqua 'Setsugekka' ('Fluted White'), 54, 56
Camellia sasanqua 'Sparkling Burgundy', 27, 54–55
Camellia sasanqua 'Yuletide', 37, 55, 57, 122–123
Camellia x 'Fragrant Pink', 68–69, 71, 105, 111
Camellia x 'Pink Icicle', 54–55
Camellia x 'Showa-No-Sakae', 59
Camellia x 'Taylor's Perfection', 28, 69, 71, 73, 84
Camellia x 'Tiny Princess', 75
Cannon, Mildred, 15, 16
Cape jasmine, 111
Cemetery Gardenia, 117–118
Cephalotaxus harringtonia, 112
Ceratostigma plumbaginoides, 110
Channell, Lula, 95, 96
Channell, Mary Carolyn (Carrie), 96
Cherokee rose, 23, 85
Cherry laurel, 23
Chinese snowball, 23, 48, 50
Chinese wisteria, 128
Chionanthus virginicus, 23, 111
Christmas rose, 27
Clematis, 26, 85
Clematis armandii, 21–22
Clematis 'Henryi', 85

INDEX

Clematis 'Jackmanii', 91
Climbing hydrangea, 62, 65
Cold Harbor, Virginia, 96
Columbine, 109
Commercial High School, Atlanta, Georgia, 15–16
Confederate jasmine, 24
Confederate rose, 27
Cornus kousa, 27, 129
Corylopsis, 32
Cotinus coggygria 'Royal Purple', 37, 90, 91
Crocosmia sp., 111

D

Daffodil, 27, 83, 127–128
Daphne, 24, 37, 44
Daphne odora, 25–26, 77–78, 90, 112
David Austin English rose, 23–25
Daylily, 14–15, 27, 91, 102–103, 110, 131
Daylily foliage, 130–131
Dean, Elizabeth, 65
Decumaria barbara, 62
DeKalb County, Georgia, 15
Digitalis purpurea, 26
Dillard, Tara, 21, 65, 71, 77, 95
Dirr, Michael A., 50, 62–63, 124
Dogwood, 26
Doublefile viburnum, 51
Dwarf flowering almond, 22, 32, 97
Dwarf iris, 90
Dwarf mondo grass, 22

E

East Lake, 17
Edgeworthia chrysantha, 24
Elliott, Kim, 122
Elliott, Si, 122
Epimedium sp., 24, 28, 80, 84, 113
Epimedium x *versicolor* 'Sulphureum', 110
Eucomis 'Sparkling Burgundy', 78–79, 91, 112
Euonymus alatus, 22
Exbury azalea, 90
Exochorda racemosa, 98

F

Fairy wings, 110
Fallopia japonica 'Variegata', 110
Farmers and Consumers Market Bulletin, 42, 77, 97, 100
Fern, 24, 27, 62, 80
Flanders, Danny, 12
Fleece flower, 110

Florida anise, 23
Flowering apricot, 22, 27, 112
Foxglove, 26–27

G

Garden phlox, 27
Gardener's Diary, A, 9–10, 12, 41, 44–45, 106, 124
Gardenia, 24–25, 113, 129,
Gardenia jasminoides, 111
Gardening for Love, 97
Georgia Perennial Plant Association, 85, 105
Geranium maculatum, 110
Ginkgo biloba, 121
Ginkgo leaves, 116, 120–121
Ginkgo tree, 22, 25, 120–121, 129
Gladiolus sp., 98
Glasener, Erica, 124–125
Golden creeping Jenny, 110
'Goldheart' English ivy, 128
Grancy graybeard, 23, 111
Green Brothers Nursery, 64
Greene County, Georgia, 15, 95, 96
Greensboro, Georgia, 15
Griffith, Gene, 65
Gumpo azalea, 91

H

Halesia diptera, 23, 35, 78–79
Hall's Garden Center, 77
Hardy begonia, 17, 110
Hardy gladiolus, 23, 42, 98
Hardy plumbago, 110
Hardy terrestrial orchid, 110
Harris, Carol, 134
Hastings, 15
Hellebore, 24, 37, 84, 92, 113
Helleborus niger, 27
Helleborus x *hybridus*, 27, 43–44, 90, 110–111
Hemerocallis 'Lullabye Baby', 89, 110
Henry County, Georgia, 98
Hibiscus mutabilis, 27
Hibiscus syriacus, 111
Hibiscus syriacus 'Bluebird', 82
Hippeastrum x *johnsonii*, 98
Holly, 128
Holly fern, 68
Home & Garden Television, 9–10, 41, 44–45, 106
'Honorine Jobert' Japanese anemone, 25
Hosta, 24, 62, 80, 92, 112
Hosta 'Blue Angel', 68, 90
Hosta 'Patriot', 79
Hosta 'Sagae', 79, 90

INDEX

Hosta 'Sum and Substance', 25, 128–129
Hosta 'White Christmas', 79
Hosta x 'Royal Standard', 111
Houttuynia, 128
Hudson, Susanne, 32
Hydrangea, 22, 24–25, 27, 34, 36, 38–39, 47, 62, 64, 66–67, 80, 90, 101, 106, 112, 117, 124, 130
Hydrangea arborescens 'Annabelle', 43, 62, 63, 106, 112, 130–131
Hydrangea.com, 65
Hydrangea macrophylla, 62, 111
Hydrangea macrophylla 'Ayesha', 126–127
Hydrangea macrophylla 'Lady in Red', 63, 124–125
Hydrangea macrophylla 'Margaret Moseley', 24, 64–65, 113, 134
Hydrangea macrophylla 'Mini Penny', 62
Hydrangea macrophylla 'Mme. Émile Moulière', 65
Hydrangea macrophylla 'Penny Mac', 62–63
Hydrangea macrophylla 'Pia', 112
Hydrangea macrophylla 'Sister Theresa', 65
Hydrangea macrophylla 'Twist-n-Shout', 63
Hydrangea paniculata, 62–63
Hydrangea paniculata 'Grandiflora', 65
Hydrangea paniculata 'Tardiva', 27, 65
Hydrangea quercifolia, 62, 67
Hydrangea quercifolia 'Snowflake', 33, 111
Hydrangea serrata 'Blue Billow', 111
Hydrangea serrata 'Bluebird', 62
Hydrangea serrata 'Fuji Waterfall', 66–67
Hydrangea x 'Preziosa', 41, 62, 112

I

Ilex latifolia hybrid, 'Emily Brunner', 27, 33
Impatiens, 100
International Clematis Society, 105
Ipheion uniflorum, 99
Iris, 22, 78, 110
Iris 'Beverly Sills', 25, 76–77
Iris ensata 'Summer Storm', 89
Iris germanica, 110
Iris japonica, 131
Itea virginica 'Henry's Garnet', 33

J

Jacob's Ladder gladiolus, 98
Japanese aster, 24, 42, 110
Japenese iris, 89
Japenese lantern, 9
Japenese maple, 121
Japenese painted fern, 109–110
Japenese paper plant, 24
Japenese plum yew, 25, 37
Japenese Solomon's seal, 54

Jefferson, Thomas, 97
Jonas, Sandra, 71, 86, 89, 113
Jones, Jeane, 68, 96, 107–108

K

Kalimeris pinnatifida 'Hortensis', 42–43, 110
Kerria, 22
Korean lilac, 27
Korean spice viburnum, 49
Kousa dogwood, 129
Kwanzan cherry tree, 22

L

Lacy, Allen, 97
Lamb's ear, 110–111
Lamium maculatum 'Beacon Silver', 110
Land Arts Nursery, 108, 113
Larkspur, 27, 129
Lawrence, Elizabeth, 40–44, 97, 128
Lee, Gen. Robert E., 96
Lee, Susan Carter, portraitist, 132–133
Lenten rose, 27, 43–44, 110–111
Leyland cypress, 23
Linden viburnum, 48
Liriope muscari 'Variegata', 110
Lunaria annua, 100–101
Lysimachia nummularia 'Aurea', 110
Lythrum salicaria, 110

M

Magnolia grandiflora, 79
Maidenhair fern, 68, 90, 110
Marchman, Thomas Jefferson "Fox", 96
Mariana maiden fern, 24, 100, 110
'Martha's Dream' sasanqua, 27
Martin, Bud, 79, 81, 90
'Mary's Gold' daylily, 17
Master Gardener, 10, 81, 106, 124
McGuinn, Phyllis, 47, 113
McHenry, Penny, 62, 71, 104–105
Michelia maudiae, 25, 79, 85, 124
Money plant, 24
Montbretia, 111

N

Narcissus, 83
Native azalea, 23, 88–89

INDEX

O

Oakleaf hydrangea, 91
Okame cherry, 27
Ophiopogon planiscapus 'Nigrescens', 110
Oxalis, 110
Oxydendrum arboreum, 122–123

P

Paeonia 'Festiva Maxima', 99
Pansies, 27
Papaver somniferum var. *paeoniflorum*, 110
Parrot Lily, 99, 110
Peacock fern, 110
Pearlbush, 22, 98
Peonies, 22, 78, 95
Petunia, 25, 89
Phlox divaricata, 91, 130, 131
Pieris, 84
Pieris japonica, 22, 69, 80
Pike Family Nurseries, 75
Pineapple sage, 22
Pine tree, 18, 128–129
Plum yew, 112
Pomegranate, 23, 86–87
Poppy, 23, 36, 97, 110, 112, 129, 132
Portrait, "Margaret in Her Garden", 132–133
Potter, Jeff, 118
Prunus glandulosa, 32
Prunus glandulosa 'Alba', 97
Prunus mume, 22, 27, 66–67, 71, 112, 129
Purple loosestrife, 110
Purple smoketree, 22–23, 37, 90–91

R

Rhododendron, 18, 22–24
Rhododendron 'Anna Rose Whitney', 33, 80
Rhododendron poukhanense 'Corsage', 11
Rhododendron 'Roseum Elegans', 25, 80, 89
Rodriguez, Fidel, 134
Rosa 'Graham Stuart Thomas', 23
Rosa 'Heritage', 23
Rosa laevigata, 23, 85
Rosa 'Mutabilis', 22, 112
Rosa 'The Pilgrim', 23
Rose, 36, 80–81, 94–95, 111
Rose of Sharon, 82

S

Sasanqua, 24, 61, 128
Sassafras leaf, 122–123
Sassafras tree, 122
Schizophragma hydrangeoides 'Moonlight', 62, 65, 112
Scilla hispanica, 24–25, 28
Sedum, 92
Sedum sieboldii, 110
Selaginella braunii, 110
Selaginella uncinata, 110
'Shady Lady' daylily, 100
Siberian iris, 23
Silverbell tree, 35
'Snowflake' oakleaf hydrangea, 23
Sourwood tree, 122–123
Southeastern Flower Show, 43, 84, 118
Southern Garden, A Handbook for the Middle South, A, 40–43
Southern Living 2001 Garden Annual, 10–11
Southern Living Garden Book, 10–11
Southern Living magazine, 10–11, 94, 106–107, 108
Spiraea x *bumalda* 'Goldflame', 88–89
Spiraea 'Fujino Pink', 84
Spirea, 23, 37, 84
Spring starflower, 99
Stachys byzantina, 110–111
State Flower of Georgia, 85
St. Joseph's Lily, 98
Stokes' aster, 110
Stokesia laevis, 110
Stonecrop, 110
Stout Medal, 17
St. Simons Island, Georgia, 41, 49
'Sum and Substance' hosta, 25
Styrax japonicus, 112

T

Tea olive, 85
Tea viburnum, 51
The Charlotte Observer, 41
Thelypteris torresiana, 100, 110
Toad lily, 85
Tricyrtis sp., 85
Tulip, 27

V

Variegated Japanese knotweed, 110
Variegated liriope, 110
Veazey, Georgia, 15, 95
Viburnum, 22–23, 25–26, 44, 47–49, 85

INDEX

Viburnum carlesii, 49, 112
Viburnum dilatatum 'Erie', 48
Viburnum macrocephalum, 9, 11, 23, 48, 50–52, 112
Viburnum plicatum forma 'Popcorn', 50
Viburnum plicatum 'Kern's Pink', 53
Viburnum plicatum var. *tomentosum* 'Shasta', 12, 51
Viburnum setigerum, 51
Viburnum utile, 50
Viburnum utile 'Eskimo', 50
Viburnums: Flowering Shrubs for Every Season, 50
Viburnum x *burkwoodii* 'Mohawk', 49–50
Viburnum x *carlcephalum*, 49–50, 112
Viburnum x *carlcephalum* 'Cayuga', 50
Viburnum x *juddii*, 49

W

Walker Nursery Farms, 71
Ward, Gloria, 113
Wayside Gardens, 49, 82
Weathers, Mike, 134
White flowering quince, 22
Wild geranium, 110
Wilkerson Mill Gardens, 65
Winterhazel, 22, 32
Wisteria, 128
Wormwood, 110

Y

Yeager, Marsha, 113
Yellow creeping Jenny, 25